POWERSHOP
NEW JAPANESE RETAIL DESIGN

Birkhäuser – Publishers for Architecture
Basel • Boston • Berlin

Frame Publishers
Amsterdam

IMAGINATION REIGNS

A book on shopping in Japan could not possibly begin without a reference, however brief, to the country's recent economic history. A hot topic of global interest in the latter part of the 20th century was Japan's 'bubble economy', a term used to define the period of fabulous growth that carried the nation to unknown heights between the late 1960s and, to be exact, the final day of 1989. Thriving as never before, Japan experienced a rapid international business expansion. Politicians, executives and white-collar workers – the suits in charge – focused on one thing only: the greatest possible market share. The degree of dedication that organisations expected from their employees sometimes led to housing located on company premises. The rewards were substantial: everyone profited from a glowing economic climate.

The ride lasted right up to the last day of 1989, when the system revealed its foundations to be no more than an air bubble. The economy collapsed, one bankruptcy followed another, corruption scandals surfaced, and unemployment rose. What followed was, economically speaking, a pitch-black period that is still waiting for a light to appear at the end of the tunnel.

Slump or no slump, however, Japan is and remains a perfect example of 'the consumer society'. As a favoured leisure activity, shopping is surpassed only by listening to music, driving cars and singing karaoke. The average Japanese has an insatiable appetite for labels, is extremely fashion conscious and has no qualms about spending money to satisfy material cravings.

Fed by uncertainties, however, the buying public has become increasingly unpredictable. This is reflected in the street scene. Once the realm of grey business suits, Japan is now the stage for the most widely divergent clothing styles. Nowhere else do young people go to such ends to express their personalities through bizarre hairdos, wild fashions and an endless array of gadgets. And the speed at which styles change in Japan borders on the incredible. Interested? Take a stroll down www.j-streetstyle.com, a website that offers monthly reports on street styles in five trendy Tokyo districts. Tokyo has certainly earned the title 'Capital of Streetwear'.

The pressing desire for a new look is fuelled by an incredibly large and varied number of fashion and lifestyle shops. Cities like Tokyo, Osaka and Kyoto teem with often obscure establishments that exude an underground ambience. Each shop reflects the style of the street: they have the same rather bizarre look that marks their clientele, and they transform their interiors more frequently than any other type of store. When a shop – often an outlet for a single streetwear brand – is a hit, long queues line the pavement outside. The less successful shop, however, is mercilessly subjected to a total renovation. Or it drops out of the picture – trend over, game over.

All the big fashion chains represented in Japan have not only a Japanese flagship store, but also a fleet of satellites and shops-in-shops. Compared with their cousins in Paris, London and Milan, designer shops here are far more approachable. Customers are younger and more capricious. Big-name brands that want to make it in the Land of the Rising Sun cannot ignore the law of the street: every detail of their shops must reflect what the label stands for. And if an interior threatens to become boring or obsolete – something that can easily happen within three to five years – the doors close, only to open after a short interruption of operations to introduce a fresh and intriguing interior.

It's safe to say that Japan's retail designers are unrivalled as professionals obliged to respond to current trends. The situation gives them the opportunity to design artistic, even fantastic retail environments. At first glance, these shops may not look very commercial. But appearances are deceiving. Every retail designer prioritises the interest of his client: the wish to sell as much as possible. If his design fails to create the right conditions for sales, he's soon out of business.

All ten designers featured in this book are masters at maintaining the balance between creativity and commerce. Even though they are active in other areas – nearly all of them

design furniture and lamps, as well as offices and restaurants, for example – each has undeniably won his spurs as a retail designer. Completely in keeping with developments in Japan, moreover, each has developed his own style and has acquired clients who favour that style. AZB, EXIT, Masamichi Katayama and Tsutomu Kurokawa often work for retailers that sell streetwear. The work of Masaru Ito, Yasuo Kondo, Gwenael Nicolas, Hideo Yasui and Tokujin Yoshioka is more suited to designer labels, such as Issey Miyake and Yohji Yamamoto. Akihito Fumita, on the other hand, has created his own niche, which is determined more by a particular lifestyle.

The designers presented here prove that a shop can resemble an art installation and still be successful. They prove that it pays to invest in creativity. And they certainly prove that in Japan – even in lean economic times – imagination reigns.

Robert Thiemann / Frame *magazine*

AZB
ETTO FRANCISCO OHASHI
TAKAMARO KOUJI AYANO

大橋 フランシスコ エット
アヤノ 工事 タカマロ

One look at the name – Allgemeine Zukünftig Büro (AZB) – strongly suggests that our destination is not an ordinary design agency, a suspicion confirmed upon arrival at the office of this Japanese design duo. Here in the upscale Tokyo neighbourhood of Denenchofu, two brothers took on the family home as one of their first projects, converting it into an office with living quarters. Eccentric furnishings (AZB designs) and sloping lead-glass windows share the premises with a casually arranged computer corner, a spacious open kitchen and an impressive bar. The result looks more like a church transformed into a café than the workplace that it is.

An overriding sense of confusion is a recurring theme in AZB's work. Takamaro Kouji Ayano (born Takaaki Ohashi) and Etto Francisco Ohashi (originally Chiaki Ohashi) love to combine seemingly incompatible styles, a strategy leading to contrasts that they see as a logical consequence of their collaborative efforts. After all, Etto the philosopher and Kouji the pragmatist view each project from different perspectives.

Their aliases allow clients to distinguish between the two. 'In Japan, it's customary to identify yourself on the phone by stating your surname,' explains Kouji. 'If I say "Ohashi", the caller isn't sure who he has on the line.' He chose his new name for its pleasing sound and because *kouji* means 'building' or 'construction' in Japanese. Etto is his brother's nickname, and Francisco refers to their Christian faith.

Kouji is the more talkative of the two. When Etto does offer an opinion, it invariably clashes with that of his brother. Both believe that their polar personalities are a vital ingredient of their teamwork: two halves in opposition form an auspicious whole. When they want a third opinion, they call on interior designer Naomi Shioura, who works with them on a regular basis. Together they create surprising objects, many of which resemble art installations more than functional pieces of furniture. Cryptic names like Peace Weapon for the Future – referring to a computer table – reinforce the artistic aspect of their work.

Founded in 1983, AZB first entered the field of furniture design and later moved into the sphere of interior design and architecture. A passion for Germany is revealed in the name they selected for their organisation. Etto is drawn to Rudolf Steiner's thorough, serious approach to his work, while Kouji moves to the beat of German techno. 'I like industrial sounds and rhythms,' he says. 'Melodies are wasted on me.' Both men are fascinated by the future – another clue to the agency's name – but certainly not to the detriment of their roots.

Although a conversation with the two initially raises more questions than it answers, a love of the traditional elements found in Japanese aesthetics and design visibly inspires their work. A major influence is 16th-century tea master Sen no Rikyu, who's left a definite mark on their projects. Rikyu took the tea ceremony back to basics. He used simple materials and reduced the area of the tearoom to a two-tatami cocoon (one tatami measures 180 x 90 cm). 'We see the Japanese teahouse as the perfect form,' says Etto. 'Although virtually bare, it's still comfortable. The teahouse is a universe that exists within a minimum of space.'

'The Japanese place a high priority on the perfection of daily activities, such as the enjoyment of tea,' his brother adds. 'In and of itself, a small space is already intimate and cosy. It's the kind of aesthetic we admire, and one that we try to recreate.' An example is the Japanese rock garden, which turns up in each of their retail projects in one form or another.

A striking example of their work is the interior design of two shops in Akita, which are separated by less than 300 metres. The menswear shop, α-Compiler, is austere, cool and futuristic, as if it just stepped out of a Japanese sci-fi manga. Kouji denies the connection to either manga or science fiction: 'All we wanted was an ultra-simple form with no superfluous details. Here's a plain, unadorned structure that a little kid might have drawn.' Automatic sliding doors – according to the designers, the first slanting entrance doors in Japan – invite visitors to step into the

'WE SEE THE JAPANESE TEAHOUSE AS THE PERFECT FORM. ALTHOUGH VIRTUALLY BARE, IT'S STILL COMFORTABLE – A UNIVERSE EXISTING WITHIN A MINIMUM OF SPACE'

future. Everything is rounded and soft. Differences in height, along with low ceilings, are both alienating and whimsical. Kouji compares it to 'being inside a huge animal,' but he could have referred just as easily to a spaceship.

The other shop, α-Assembler, sells sporty leisure fashions. Here the interior is earthy, almost traditionally Japanese and warm. At the entrance are fabric panels called *noren*, a feature of many Japanese restaurants, and the floor is covered with *doma*, or tamped-down earth, in the style of old Japanese houses. Large characters on the wall spell 'danger'. Kouji explains that the design is based on the image of a samurai, a paragon of ego and greed. Certain elements were actually designed to evoke a sense of apprehension. Inside, the colour red symbolises a tank, poised to attack.

The designers see the buildings as opposites: male and female. Assembler, a structure the shade of terracotta, is masculine. Both designs boast small, offbeat versions of the traditional Japanese garden. Marked by modern attributes, these dry rock gardens are quiet still lifes in the midst of retail reality. The designers have made space for Japanese icons in other projects as well.

Location sometimes determines the choice of materials. Detail, a shop in Kanazawa, welcomes customers with gold-leaf decorations that pay tribute to a regional tradition. Juxtaposed with an indoor garden of gravel and rocks is a tea corner whose walls are clad in gold leaf.

'Yes, it's a commercial establishment,' Kouji concedes, 'but the little tearoom gives the space a domestic air.' Although the space used for the tea ceremony fascinates them, the brothers do not practise the ritual. 'I'm sure it was the avant-garde thing to do in the 16th century,' says Kouji, 'but gradually the evolution of the ceremony ground to a halt. The venue offered people a chance to relax with friends and family. Its Western equivalent is an evening at the local espresso bar. Coffee or tea – both are loaded with enough caffeine to wake up

the dead,' he laughs. In a more serious vein he adds, 'In the manner of the traditional teahouse, the tea corner in this shop represents a moment of rest.' The long, narrow aisle was also a conscious choice. 'Because you can't walk along this corridor three or four abreast, shopping becomes a rather intimate experience.' A ceiling looming only 2 metres above floor level heightens the sense of intimacy.

Playing with dimensions intrigues the brothers. Another game of measurements is found in their @home delux project, which features the grillwork of a climbing frame. With fairly short intervals between its bars, the frame can only be entered with a little difficulty. Stairs and a small passageway form an interesting centrepiece. 'We try to put a bit of fun into each of our projects,' says Kouji.

In the long run, Etto predicts, we can expect big things from AZB, because 'to produce something really good, a person has to be 70 or 80, an age at which human emotions – love, anger, regret and grief – finally converge.' Seen in this light, their designs are no more than beginners' experiments in a lifelong search for absolute perfection. Etto humbly asks for our patience. The proof of the pudding is in *die Zukunft*.

AZB
ETTO FRANCISCO OHASHI
TAKAMARO KOUJI AYANO

大橋 フランシスコ エット
アヤノ 工事 タカマロ

α-COMPILER

LOCATION
**7-7-4 Higashi dori,
Akita-shi, Akita-ken**
CLIENT
Bellnald International
FLOOR AREA
371 m²
START DESIGN
October 1998
OPENING
25 September 1999
ARCHITECT
AZB
INTERIOR ARCHITECT
AZB
GENERAL CONSTRUCTOR
Harima Kensetsu
LIGHTING DESIGN
AZB
FLOOR
epoxy resin (second and third floor)
WALL
stainless steel
CEILING
plasterboard, aluminium honeycombs
WINDOW
glass, screen film
SEATING
stainless steel, vinly leather
SEATING FABRIC
leather
COUNTER
stainless steel
SHOWCASES
stainless steel
STAIRS
stainless steel

PHOTOGRAPHY
Nacása & Partners

α-ASSEMBLER

LOCATION
**6-18-22 Higashi dori,
Akita-shi, Akita-ken**
CLIENT
Bellnald International
FLOOR AREA
278 m²
START DESIGN
October 1998
OPENING
25 September 1999
ARCHITECT
AZB
INTERIOR ARCHITECT
AZB
GENERAL CONSTRUCTOR
Harima Kensetsu
LIGHTING DESIGN
AZB
FLOOR
**earth/clay, stainless steel, concrete (first
floor); concrete (second floor)**
WALL
**earth/clay, stainless steel, concrete (first
floor); glass, plasterboard (second floor)**
CEILING
**skeleton, stainless steel (first floor);
plasterboard (second floor)**
WINDOW
glass, film
COUNTER
steel
SHOWCASES
steel, burned Akita cedar wood
JUNGLE GYM
**steel, zinc, fibre-reinforced plastic board,
slip-resistant steel**

PHOTOGRAPHY
Nacása & Partners

DETAIL

LOCATION
**110-1 Tatemachi,
Kanazawa-shi, Ishikawa-ken**
CLIENT
S Curve Studio
FLOOR AREA
165 m²
START DESIGN
October 1999
OPENING
18 February 2000
ARCHITECT
Tadao Ando (1991)
INTERIOR ARCHITECT
AZB
GENERAL CONSTRUCTOR
Cranberrys & Associates
LIGHTING DESIGN
AZB
FLOOR
**earth/clay, concrete and paint, aluminium
foil, gravel, epoxy resin**
WALL
**earth/clay, stainless, painted wood,
epoxy resin**
CEILING
**epoxy resin, acrylic emergent paint,
plasterboard**
WINDOW
glass, film
COUNTER
painted plasterboard
SHOWCASES
glass, aluminium
CHAIR
stainless, wool
CHASHITSU SEATING ELEMENT
**Tatami rice mat, gold leaf, acrylic, stainless
steel**

PHOTOGRAPHY
Nishiguchi Toshikazu

@HOME DELUX

LOCATION
**2-38 Kaiunbashi dori,
Morioka-shi, Iwate-ken**
CLIENT
Hops Company
FLOOR AREA
880 m²
START DESIGN
November 2000
OPENING
1 September 2001
ARCHITECT
AZB
INTERIOR ARCHITECT
AZB
GENERAL CONSTRUCTOR
Marui Kenso
LIGHTING DESIGN
AZB
FLOOR
**concrete, glass light box (first floor);
concrete, slip-resistant steel (second floor);
concrete (third floor)**
WALL
**concrete, plasterboard,
fibre-reinforced plastic**
CEILING
**plasterboard (first and second floor);
plasterboard, skeleton (third floor)**
WINDOW
glass
LIGHTING FIXTURES
Daiko
SEATING
steel, fibre-reinforced plastic
JUNGLE GYM
**steel, zinc, fibre-reinforced plastic board,
slip-resistant steel**
COUNTER
teakwood, stainless steel, glass
SHOWCASES
**teakwood, stainless steel,
transparent acrylic**
HANGERS
stainless steel wire

PHOTOGRAPHY
Haruhi Fujii

AZB
1-43-17 DENENCHOFU, OTA-KU, TOKYO, 145-0071 JAPAN
T/F +81 (0)3-3721-6814
E AZB-TAKAMARO@MX8.TTCN.NE.JP

AZB
AZB
AZB
AZB
AZB
AZB
AZB
AZB
AZB
AZB
AZB
AZB
AZB
AZB
AZB
AZB
AZB
AZB
AZB
AZB
AZB
AZB
AZB
AZB
AZB
AZB
AZB
AZB
AZB
AZB
AZB
AZB
AZB
AZB
AZB
AZB
AZB
AZB
AZB
AZB
AZB
AZB
AZB
AZB
AZB
AZB
AZB
AZB
AZB
AZB
AZB
AZB
AZB
AZB
AZB
AZB
AZB
AZB
AZB
AZB
AZB
AZB
AZB

α-COMPILER

In the provincial city of Akita, AZB designed two shops separated by less than 300 metres. Although the two are each other's opposites, they are seen as an inextricable pair. Austere, cool and futuristic, α-Compiler looks like a spaceship that's just landed on the pages of a Japanese sci-fi manga. Clad in easy-maintenance FRP (fibre-reinforced plastic), the off-white building steals the show in downtown Akita. AZB wanted to create an ultra-simple form with no superfluous details and, using the traditional culture of Japan as a point of departure, to sketch an image of the future. Automatic sliding entrance doors that slant backwards are, according to the designers, the first of their kind in Japan. (Note: Although accessed by these doors, the Paul Smith outlet at ground level is not an AZB design.) Most display units on the first floor are made of stainless steel, including the honeycomb shelves. Certain units are incorporated into the surface of the floor, while others resembling large illuminated refrigerators line the walls. Everything is rounded and soft. A Japanese rock garden features Catseyes. Differences in height, a narrow passageway and low ceilings are both alienating and whimsical. A staircase hovering in space leads to an upper level marked by little innovation. Hangers are affixed to sturdy steel wires strung between floor and ceiling. Seated on a low bench – AZB's reference to 'super low life' – customers can view images projected on a large window overlaid with a special film. One could almost forget that this is a streetwear boutique.

α-ASSEMBLER

The second part of this dual project is α-Assembler, an earthy, warm shop that appears, at first glance, to be traditionally Japanese. This boutique is the antithesis of its partner, α-Compiler, although both specialise in streetwear for men. The entrance is enhanced by fabric panels called *noren*, a feature of many Japanese restaurants, and an old lantern stands next to the entrance path. Inside, the floor is simply tamped-down earth, or *doma*. Despite details in bamboo, however, the sense of being in ancient Japan soon subsides. Blood-red walls and stainless-steel surfaces are rather fierce, in-your-face elements. Waiting at the end of a tunnel flanked by rows of hanging clothes is an illuminated ventilator accompanied by the Japanese word for 'danger'. AZB based the design on the image of a samurai, whose ego, greed and macho temperament find expression in this angular, robust interior. A small café upstairs is furnished with AZB products. On the café windows, layers of film in various colours enliven the sterile white space. The exterior of the building is primarily the colour of terracotta. A rusty fence made of perforated scrap metal effectively divides shop and street, while also making an attractive addition to the design.

DETAIL

In designing Detail, another shop that
features casual fashions, AZB decided
to incorporate a number of traditional
Japanese icons into the space.
Located on a modern shopping street in
Kanazawa, Detail is fronted by a loamed
porch with stepping stones that lead to
an 'aisle shop' bathed in bright yellow
light. AZB's aim was to create a cosy
cocoon, low and narrow. Built-in display
cases alternate with seating for two.
A stainless-steel strip halfway down
the aisle accentuates the entrance to
a fitting room and an indoor rock garden
that offers more than the eye can take
in at first glance. A turntable filled with
carefully raked white gravel pierces
a carved-out rock. Water trickles from
a lead pipe set into the opening of another
rock into a reservoir with a red light at
its centre. Black light falling on small
tables and one-legged chairs forms
a contemporary contrast to the primeval
rocks. Coated in blue film, perforated
scrap metal along the wall combines
with film-clad windows to produce
a bizarre space with a rather psychedelic
atmosphere. Aglow with gold leaf,
walls at the back of the shop refer to
the traditional Japanese teahouse,
or chashitsu. This area functions not
only as a haven for weary shoppers,
but also as an icon for Kanazawa,
an important centre of culture with a rich
history in the processing of gold leaf.
Tatami mats set into the teahouse walls
serve as chairs. Such a generous supply
of seating is particularly welcome in a
colourful shop bursting with an avalanche
of accents that take a good deal of time
and concentration to appreciate fully.

@HOME DELUX

This four-storey-high concrete building on a busy shopping street in the northern Japanese city of Morioka looks like an ordinary department store with a large corner display window. A glance inside reveals a huge climbing frame that reaches the ceiling. What's this? An indoor playground? Not at all. It's a multi-tenant building for casual-wear boutiques. AZB's designers used the eye-catching framework as a basis for designing this far-from-ordinary store. Mat-glass screens, which provide a backdrop for displaying fashions and accessories, prevent visitors from actually scaling the apparatus for a better look at the ceiling. The installation is, in fact, a labyrinth that extends upwards through two shops, one on the ground floor and another above. On the way up, seats offer a place for those in need of a breather. Big jerry cans with built-in lighting are a nice complement to the illuminated floor.

Although the climbing frame is the highlight of the building, the side entrance boasts another surprising element – a cubiform tunnel floating 10 centimetres above the ground. A high staircase at the centre of the building leads to two more shops, where wooden display units covered in a wood-grain film radiate the spirit of the 1950s. Check out the collection of T-shirts on hangers virtually suspended in space, or step into a fitting cubicle dazzling with light. This exclusive selection of shops sells brands like Stüssy, Nike, Revolver and X-large. With their love of Japanese gardens, the AZB designers simply couldn't resist adding a rock garden to the interior, complete with a water feature.

CURIOSITY
GWENAEL NICOLAS

グエナエル ニコラ

Designer Gwenael Nicolas and marketeer Reiko Miyamoto are the faces behind the four-year-old design studio Curiosity. Although the Frenchman and his Japanese partner maintain an office in an ordinary shopping street like many others, one glance at the nearby skyscrapers of Shinjuku brings with it the realisation that this is the heart of Tokyo.

The ground-floor space that functions as both gallery and conference room has been transformed into a mock-up of the latest project. Backed by experience as a product designer, creative brain Nicolas knows as no other that between drawing board and production lies a highly instructive phase: the construction of a prototype.

I'm looking at one of Curiosity's bigger projects to date: the interior design of four shops for timepiece titan Tag Heuer. Understandably, Nicolas would rather be safe than sorry. The space is filled with the complicated, full-scale contrivances that are his guinea pigs. At first glance it all looks set to go, but open tool boxes and a snarl of cables in one corner show that the operation is poised in midstream.

Eye-catchers are walnut panelling with spaces cut out to hold transparent cubes, thick glass sliding doors fronting beautifully illuminated display cases and a less-than-perfect display behind black glass. 'Fortunately, we still have time to polish the act before it opens,' says Nicolas. Sounding like a practised peddler of watches, he points out clever details in the design.

'I approach an interior as though it were a product,' he says. 'The first step is to see how the space looks from the outside. Then I try to imagine the effect that light, volume and materials will have on this particular interior. The nice thing about any space is its capacity to arouse emotions. It's an experience. A product doesn't have the same sort of impact.'

The spoken words reveal his strength. The Frenchman experiments with products and the context in which they are displayed. He combines function and aesthetics. Already tinkering with design as a teenager, he focused on surfboards, which he

made by hand and then sold. He wanted to craft a super-cool product that would skim over the waves at lightning speeds. Form equals function. In the wake of seeing Star Wars, he decided to become a designer. 'My dream was to convert the imaginary world of the silver screen into reality. It's so easy to design spectacular things. The real challenge lies in getting your ideas realised and in making sure that people actually buy and use them.'

After completing his education in interior design in Paris, Nicolas took off for London, where he studied product design at the Royal College of Arts. It was there that he became fascinated with Japanese design and, consequently, selected a trip to Tokyo as his prize for the design of an aeroplane seat for British Airways.

During his first few years in Japan, he concentrated on product design. It wasn't long, however, before he joined Waterstudio, a well-known agency headed by Naoki Sakai, from whom he learned the tricks of the trade. 'He taught me not to take my job as a designer too seriously,' Nicolas recalls with a grin. Among his projects for Sakai were futuristic telephones and audio equipment for clients like Lucky Goldstar and Panasonic.

The first commission labelled 'Gwenael Nicolas' was for the design of a modern *butsudan*, a mini temple in honour of the dead, which has a place in nearly every Japanese household. 'Strange how that goes,' he says. 'You study so many things and voilà – your first commission is something totally different.' A lovely combination of modern and traditional structures, his simple but tasteful design later brought him into contact with Issey Miyake. Fascinated by the *butsudan*, the fashion designer famed for his daring use of materials and intriguing shops threw Nicolas headfirst into the world of retail design. The day after they met, Miyake asked him to design a shop in Paris, the first of a series of outlets he has created for the fashion guru. In the meantime, Nicolas's work as product designer continues at a steady pace, as reflected by everything from ingeniously designed scent bottles to a restyled Nintendo GameBoy. An interesting feature of the Tag Heuer project is the link between interior design and product design. Used for displaying watches,

'A SHOP SHOULD BE MORE THAN A FEAST FOR THE EYES. IF YOU DON'T PROVIDE A WAY FOR PEOPLE TO MOVE THROUGH THE SPACE, THEY WON'T SEE THE PRODUCT'

the transparent cubes revolve 90 degrees while keeping the small trays they contain perfectly horizontal. Accents like this one play a major role in the Miyake shops as well. 'I try to minimise the visible functions of a space,' says Nicolas. 'Sometimes this means transforming three dimensions into two. At other times it means combining storage space with retail space or product design with interior design.' The cheerful honeycomb in one of Miyake's Pleats Please outlets serves as both focal point and storage unit, while a huge curtain conceals the stockroom and fitting cubicles.

The prototype for Tag Heuer is an exception to the rule. Japan's interior designers seldom have time for prototypes. The country's sky-high rents force retailers to open their doors as quickly as possible. An example is the Pleats Please shop in Aoyama, a race-against-the-clock project for which Nicolas had only 30 days from design to opening. 'In a case like that,' he says, 'the designer is primarily a decision maker.' His decisions were aimed at time, money and quality.

To Nicolas, retail design is all about incorporating the intelligence of the product into the space. 'In the beginning,' he explains, 'I thought that visual impact was top priority, that a customer entering the shop had to think "wow". But I soon realised that "wow" isn't enough. You have to provide a way for people to move through the space. It has to be more than a feast for the eyes. Without motion, they won't see the product. Furthermore, customers should be able to look at the merchandise from different perspectives. What I do now is play with the combination of impact, flow and a graphically photogenic result. The graphic aspect of a shop creates a long-lasting image in people's minds.' Graphic highlights are a feature of nearly every retail project he designs.

Nicolas admires architects like Alvaro Siza and Dominique Perrault, whose design of the Bibliothèque Nationale de France looks like a simple box: the epitome of functionalism. 'Even their most impersonal design merges with the surroundings, evokes an emotion and thus comes to life.'

When confronted with a new project, Nicolas plunges into his favourite architecture books in search of an ambience that corresponds to the new commission. 'At that moment, I'm not thinking about what the client wants. I'm just looking for the right atmosphere. It's not my own gallery I'll be working on but a shop that's out to make a profit, so I have to find an environment that will fit the bill.' He's talking about functionality with that little something extra. The Japanese have a nice term for it – plus alpha – and if anyone's an expert in adding to the basics, it's Nicolas. Putting things into perspective, he smiles and says: 'Retail design is really all about reducing one's ego.'

CURIOSITY
GWENAEL NICOLAS

グエナエル ニコラ

PLEATS PLEASE (MARUNOUCHI)

LOCATION
3-4-1 Marunouchi, Chiyoda-ku,
Tokyo
CLIENT
Issey Miyake
FLOOR AREA
100 m²
START DESIGN
May 1999
OPENING
July 1999
INTERIOR ARCHITECT
Gwenael Nicolas
GENERAL CONSTRUCTOR
Ishimaru
LIGHTING DESIGN
Gwenael Nicolas
FLOOR
stone, steel, slip-resistant surfing spray (yellow cube)
WALL
paint, painted steel
CEILING
paint
WINDOW
glass, film
LIGHTING FIXTURES
Max Ray
SHOWCASE
stainless polish
BENCH
stainless polish
HONEYCOMB STORAGE
coloured steel

PHOTOGRAPHY
Yasuaki Yoshinaga

TAKEO KIKUCHI TWR

LOCATION
Namba city, B2, 5-1-60 Namba, Chuo-ku,
Osaka-shi
CLIENT
World
FLOOR AREA
380 m²
START DESIGN
December 1999
OPENING
March 2000
INTERIOR ARCHITECT
Gwenael Nicolas
GENERAL CONSTRUCTOR
Zeniya
LIGHTING DESIGN
Ushio Spax
FLOOR
teak wood, red carpet (Vorwerk)
WALL
teak wood, paint
CEILING
plasterboard, red paint, white paint
LIGHTING FIXTURES
Ushio Spax
INTERNET TOWER
stainless steel
COUNTER
painted wood, stainless steel
SPIDER SOFA
leather, steel

PHOTOGRAPHY
Shimomura Photo Office

PLEATS PLEASE (AOYAMA)

LOCATION
Minami Aoyama Place,
3-13-21 Minami Aoyama, Minato-ku,
Tokyo
CLIENT
Issey Miyake
FLOOR AREA
200 m²
START DESIGN
February 2000
OPENING
April 2000
INTERIOR ARCHITECT
Gwenael Nicolas
GENERAL CONSTRUCTOR
Ishimaru
LIGHTING DESIGN
Gwenael Nicolas
FLOOR
alcelite, concrete
WALL
paint, curtain (Neoprene)
CEILING
alcelite, paint
WINDOW
glass
LIGHTING FIXTURES
Ushio Spax
STOOL
steel
COUNTER
alcelite
SHOWCASE
transparent acrylic
SOFA
elastic fabric cover
ACCESSORY TABLE
acrylic

PHOTOGRAPHY
Shinicho Sato

ME ISSEY MIYAKE

LOCATION
Matsuya Ginza, 3F,
3-6-1 Ginza, Chuo-ku,
Tokyo
CLIENT
Issey Miyake
FLOOR AREA
19 m²
START DESIGN
November 2000
OPENING
February 2001
INTERIOR ARCHITECT
Gwenael Nicolas
GENERAL CONSTRUCTOR
Ishimaru
LIGHTING DESIGN
Gwenael Nicolas
FLOOR
concrete
WALL
painted plasterboard, glass
CEILING
paint
WINDOW
glass
LIGHTING FIXTURES
Ushio Spax
VENDING DISPENSER
transparent acrylic
COUNTER
white acrylic
HANGER
transparent acrylic

PHOTOGRAPHY
Yasuaki Yoshinaga

TAG HEUER

LOCATION
5-8-1 Jingumae, Shibuya-ku, Tokyo
CLIENT
Tag Heuer
FLOOR AREA
164 m²
START DESIGN
September 2000
OPENING
October 2001
INTERIOR ARCHITECT
Gwenael Nicolas
GENERAL CONSTRUCTOR
Ishimaru
LIGHTING DESIGN
Gwenael Nicolas
FLOOR
walnut wood, alcelite
WALL
walnut wood, black glass
CEILING
plasterboard, paint
WINDOW
glass
LIGHTING FIXTURES
Ushio Spax
SPIDER CHAIR
leather, stainless steel
COUNTER
walnut wood
SHOWCASE
walnut wood, non-scratch acrylic
LOW TABLE
walnut wood, stainless steel
SOFA
leather

PHOTOGRAPHY
Nacása & Partners (Daichi Ano)

CURIOSITY
2-45-7 HONMACHI, SHIBUYA-KU, TOKYO, 151-0071 JAPAN
T +81 (0)3-5333-8525 F +81 (0)3-5371-1219
E INFO@CURIOSITY.CO.JP WWW.CURIOSITY.CO.JP

PLEATS PLEASE (MARUNOUCHI)

A metal cube painted canary yellow is the focal point of the shop, both literally and figuratively. Mounted on the ornament are a counter and a small bench. Designer Gwenael Nicolas used the yellow hulk to frame another centrally positioned eye-catcher – a brightly coloured honeycomb – this time at the rear of the boutique. This hexagonally faceted partition functions as an elegant storage unit for Issey Miyake's casual line: Pleats Please. Nicolas cleverly integrated the storage function, hidden away in most retail outlets, into a cheerful installation that is an unqualified part of the design. The interior breathes the same enthusiastic air of freshness that permeates so many of Miyake's collections. Pleats Please Marunouchi is located in a former business district currently earmarked as an upcoming fashion centre. The bustling Tokyo Station is within walking distance. The Miyake shop contributes in no small way to brightening up this rather drab neighbourhood.

TAKEO KIKUCHI TWR

In Namba, a massive underground shopping mall in the heart of Osaka, the entrance to the Takeo Kikuchi boutique is a nearly open façade. Openness aside, however, flanking black walls and low-key lighting pose a barrier.
A gigantic red box suspended from the ceiling screens the front part of the shop. This 'mask' is precisely what designer Gwenael Nicolas had in mind. By drawing attention to the ceiling, he manages to lure the observer into the central area of the shop, where most of the products are on display.
Small openings in a white wall offer a peek at fire-engine-red showcases. Peering through these spyholes, customers can spot little metal ladders or video graphics.

At the rear of the shop a deep-pile red carpet draws attention to the floor, which in the rest of the shop is a simple wooden surface. Seated on a sofa designed by Nicolas and surrounded by a suspended stainless-steel grille, customers try on exclusive Takeo Kikuchi footwear. An outlet like this one provides them with a comprehensive 'head, shoulders, knees and toes' experience. A rather fanciful design is the ingenious shelving system for suits and accessories, which features a tie display that revolves like a lazy Susan.
In addition to fashions and footwear, the shop offers an array of gadgets and other 'must-haves'.

PLEATS PLEASE (AOYAMA)

Issey Miyake wanted a marketplace
atmosphere for his Pleats Please shop
in Aoyama. Located on one of the few
shopping squares in this fashionable
Tokyo neighbourhood, the shop boasts
an interior immersed in natural light.
Apart from a striking curtain that covers
one wall of the shop, Miyake's fashions
are the only source of colour.
Today the drape is pink, but its hue
changes from season to season.
The fascinating part of this functional
space lies in the details. A good example
is the silver-grey floor at ground level,
which is repeated one floor higher in
a silvery ceiling that caps a virtually
identical space. Nicolas created
transparent tables and stools in varying
heights for the display of accessories.
Nothing distracts the customer's
attention from the vivid fashions, with
the exception of a ground-floor 'bridge'
designed to give customers a shaky
walk to their destination. Gasps of
astonishment are followed by nervous
giggles as visitors realise it's all part of
the shopping experience.
Deciding whether to cross the bridge
or descend a flight of stairs is the instant
dilemma that faces a visitor entering
the shop. Nicolas wanted the result to
be a dynamic space that makes people
want to browse around and touch the
merchandise. From the look of things on
a typical weekday – a flock of customers
inspect, reflect and select – he seems to
have achieved his goal.

ME ISSEY MIYAKE

Vending machines are a Japanese obsession. If it exists, it's probably available in a Japanese vending machine. Everything imaginable, from soft drinks and instant noodles to train tickets and magazines – not to mention live beetles and worn knickers – is stocked in one of the country's 5.6 million automated dispensers. Inspired by this phenomenon, Gwenael Nicolas used it in his retail concept for Issey Miyake's latest fashion statement: ME. In the Matsya department store in the Ginza (Tokyo), a diminutive shop-in-a-shop less than 20 metres square features a Perspex wall that looks like an oversize vending machine. Its contents are stretchy, brightly coloured tops packaged in plastic (PET) tubes. The vending-machine metaphor emphasises the mass-produced aspect of Miyake's new design. Thanks to the extreme elasticity of the fabric, the one-size-only top fits virtually every woman. These items are prepackaged at the factory, and the see-through tube, another Nicolas design, has a large screw top and an embossed, transparent logo. In the shop, a diagonally positioned rack holds sample tops, which the client can try on in a fold-out fitting cubicle. Having made her choice, she removes a tube from the transparent wall, which disperses its contents one at a time. Ultra-bright lighting has a dazzling effect on the fluorescent details of the clothing. A small recess in the round counter keeps the tube from rolling away while the customer pays. In this compact shop, every square centimetre counts.

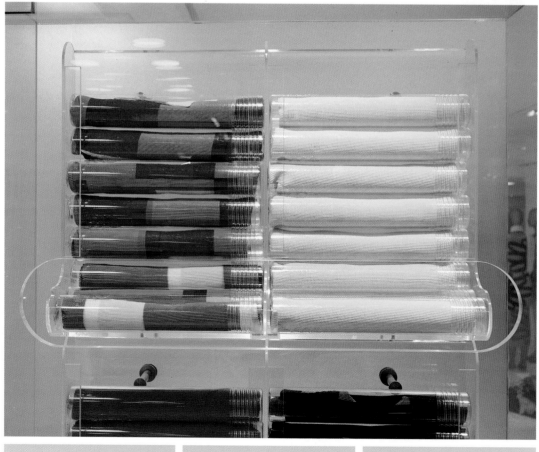

TAG HEUER

In planning the Tag Heuer façade on
Omotesando, Tokyo's only real 'strut-
your-stuff' street and Japan's nod to
the Champs Elysées, the French-born
designer opted for a graphic look.
A 4-metre-high glazed shop front offers
an interior view of several cubes and
two oversized, semitransparent blue
glass walls adjacent to stairs that take
customers to the upper floor.
Because the client wanted the shop to
reflect the exclusive yet sporty image of
the watches on display, Gwenael Nicolas
incorporated the distinguishing features
of the product into the interior. He built
installations to house the mechanical
systems and, in an attempt to slow
the pace, designed a simple space that
invites customers to zoom in on the
charm of the products.
A stroll through the shop reveals the soul
of a designer who loves subtle details.
A good example is the counter at the
rear of the shop, which seems to hover
in midair thanks to a support made of
acrylic resin. Not simply an arbitrary
choice, this transparent element is
accentuated by a band of stainless steel
inlaid in the walnut counter. It's the
perfect solution, from every angle.
The showcase cubes are another case
in point. Although they move, the rocking
motion of the trays of watches inside
is so slight that the products remain
perfectly horizontal. Another fine detail
is the lock, which is visible only for the
moment it takes to remove a watch from
the cube. And openings in a wall of black
glass reveal intriguing glimpses of a group
of watches positioned on a turntable
(featuring semi-opaque film) behind
the wall. Each display case is a separate
element. The impression created by
a wooden case fronted by two tall, glass
sliding doors suspended from the ceiling
is one of valuable timepieces there
for the taking. A closer look, however,
reveals that the space between doors
and showcase is a sliver too small for
a human hand. An air of aloofness rises
from the silvery mat floor to complement
the chic ambience created by the smooth
curve of a classic walnut wall. At the rear
of the shop a glass partition covered in
blue film subtly separates the VIP lounge
– a space both aloof and chic – from
the rest of the shop.

EXIT METAL WORK SUPPLY
TAKAO KATSUTA
KAORU SHIMIZU

勝田 隆夫
清水 薫

One visit to the studio of EXIT Metal Work Supply and the client gets the picture. An interior without metal is out of the question. Metalworking activities take place on the ground floor, where three guys are welding a railing as we walk in. Kaoru Shimizu, one of the founders of EXIT, removes his goggles and takes us upstairs. We catch a glimpse of the first-floor design department on our way to the conference room above, where he and co-founder Takao Katsuta are to be interviewed.

EXIT began in 1996 as a five-man show. It wasn't long before they were known as an ambitious team of go-getters in their mid-twenties, a rather unconventional group that pooled their talents in a gigantic workshop. With no desire to restrict themselves to retail and office interiors, they entered the field of product design as well.

'A computer table we made for a friend was our introduction to product design,' Shimizu recalls. 'Before that, computer tables were rather dark, boring objects. You can imagine the excitement generated by the bright plastic designs we made for E&Y. When the colourful, transparent iMac was launched a short time later, our sales took off. We've actually sold about 10 million yens' worth [88,000 Euros] of tables and chairs.' They called the new line of office furniture Frastic, giving a typically Japanese twist to the English language by combining the words 'frosted' and 'plastic'. 'Afterwards,' he adds, 'we accepted almost every job we were offered, but that doesn't happen any more.' EXIT is no longer interested in picking every apple on the tree, so to speak. What counts is designing and making provocative objects and spaces.

This decision conforms to the altered composition of the group. Three of the original members are gone, leaving Katsuta and Shimizu alone at the helm. Shimizu sees it as a natural process. 'After working together daily for four years, you realise that each person tackles a project differently. We all move to the beat of our own drum. Katsuta and I wanted to professionalise the work at a faster pace than the others did. The team didn't split up in anger. We're still friends. Today, however, we're all free

to follow our own ideas.' EXIT is still a relatively young, spirited outfit, but the casual nature of that earlier approach has given way to a no-nonsense working environment that zips along at an accelerated pace. The vast workshop of the early days has become a stretch of expressway, and the freewheeling atmosphere that once dominated this space is only a memory. EXIT currently focuses all its energy on a combination of interior design and metalwork.

'Metal is superior to virtually every other material,' claims Shimizu, who acquired his basic training as a metal craftsman in a factory. Later, as an employee of furniture maker Idée, he learned to prepare furniture for production, while also becoming familiar with the technical aspects of retail design. His recital of the advantages of metal has a lyrical ring: 'It's strong yet malleable, and even a thin piece of metal can take a good pounding without breaking. It's simple to repair and easy to fuse together. You can perforate metal and cover it with all sorts of coatings. You can roughen it, polish it, use it to create something stark and cool or, if you like, something rugged and rusty. Need I go on?'

Who does what at EXIT is fairly obvious. Wearing overalls custom-designed by a friend in the fashion industry, Shimizu supervises metalworking and manufacturing, while Katsuta fulfils the role of interior designer. 'For about a year before becoming an architecture student, I worked part time for an antique dealer,' says Katsuta, who sports a black T-shirt ablaze with the message 'listen to the silence'. 'Fixing up all sorts of old furniture ultimately led to my decision to become a designer. After graduating, I joined a design agency. Some of the projects I worked on brought me into regular contact with Shimizu and the other members of the original team. That's how it began.'

Katsuta is a big fan of Donald Judd, well-known minimalist sculptor and aluminium enthusiast, and he also admires the work of Jasper Morrison and lighting artist James Turrell. In reviewing his own sources of inspiration, Shimizu mentions early work by Tom Dixon as well as that of compatriot Shiro Kuramata.

'WE WANT OUR SHOP INTERIORS TO PULL VISITORS INTO A FIELD OF TENSION, TO MAKE THEM IMMEDIATELY AWARE THAT THE SPACE THEY'VE ENTERED IS NO ORDINARY SPACE'

'We try to limit the amount of design in our work,' says Katsuta. 'We want our shop interiors to pull visitors into a field of tension, as it were, to make them immediately aware that the space they've entered is no ordinary space. But creating an effect is not an end in itself. After all, the keyword is sales.' Only after making a careful study of the product line does the designer begin shaping an ambience that matches the merchandise. Number (N)ine clothing shops, for example, target the macho type who fancies a casual image – a rather offbeat, underground look. Each outlet has a different owner, and each owner consults with both fashion designer and interior architect in determining the appearance of the shop in question. Katsuta sighs. 'This ménage à trois can trap the retail designer between a rock and a hard place.' The final result, however, is a diversified series of shops that quite clearly represent a single fashion label.

'The hardest thing about designing shops is the budget,' he continues. 'It's not always possible to estimate the cost of certain components.' Katsuta draws great satisfaction though from producing an exciting space with minimum funds, as in the case of the Number (N)ine outlet in Ebisu.

Shimizu's greatest challenge to date was the suit of armour that currently greets customers to the Ebisu shop. Originally used to jazz up a fashion show, the hulk monopolised the metalworker's mind for at least a month before he solved all the problems involved. He sawed, bent, sweated and, finally, assembled more than a thousand parts into a movable contraption. 'Thanks to my knowledge of aikido,' he says, 'I understand how the body moves.' He laughingly recalls the incredible relief he felt when the project was over: 'I was sure it would kill me.'

Shimizu's passion for metal weaves through the conversation like a recurring melody. When asked to come up with a sensational example of retail design, he mentions almost immediately the aluminium tunnel at Comme des Garçons in New York. 'Making that tunnel was no picnic,' he says with conviction. 'I take my hat off to the person responsible.' He readily admits that any design featuring metal grabs his attention at once.

Nonetheless, Shimizu assures us that metal often shares the spotlight with other materials. In the majority of their projects, he and his partner collaborate with specialists who work with leather, wood and plastics. EXIT's advantage lies in the duo's manufacturing experience. 'We like the idea of being able to manufacture what we design. Thanks to that combination, our feet are planted firmly on the ground. It's a good reality check.'

Although furniture design has taken a back seat at the moment, it hasn't dropped out of the picture altogether. 'We're currently working on a shop that will be a base for selling a variety of furniture, including our own designs,' Katsuta reveals. 'We'd like nothing better than to design and make everything from cash register to toilet. But finding the time is another story.'

Indeed, time is a precious commodity for designers in demand, even when they see their workplace as a home away from home. Deadlines loom. Ashtrays overflow. A stereo guarded by manga figures sends surging strains of music soaring above the din of welding. Despite all the work going on, however, the heap of seemingly abandoned baseball gloves on the bookshelf gathers no dust. Suggest an impromptu game and heads swivel. Who's pitching?

EXIT METAL WORK SUPPLY
TAKAO KATSUTA
KAORU SHIMIZU

勝田隆夫
清水 薫

NUMBER (N)INE (EBISU)

LOCATION
**2-16-6 Ebisu, Shibuya-ku,
Tokyo**
CLIENT
Kooks Co., Ltd
START DESIGN
January 2000
OPENING
May 2000
INTERIOR ARCHITECT
EXIT Metal Work Supply
GENERAL CONSTRUCTOR
D.Brain Co.
LIGHTING DESIGN
EXIT Metal Work Supply
FLOOR
concrete
WALL
concrete
CEILING
concrete
LIGHTING FIXTURES
Max Ray
ACCESSORIES
handmade armour
SHOWCASE
metal, wired glass

PHOTOGRAPHY
Kozo Takayama

NS MORIOKA

LOCATION
**Sato Building, 1F,
1-41 Kaiunbashi dori,
Morioka**
CLIENT
Beans
FLOOR AREA
73 m²
START DESIGN
February 2000
OPENING
May 2000
INTERIOR ARCHITECT
EXIT Metal Work Supply
GENERAL CONSTRUCTOR
Marui Kenso
LIGHTING DESIGN
EXIT Metal Work Supply
FLOOR
**concrete, white paint (Soph);
concrete, black paint (Number (N)ine)**
WALL
**bamboo (Soph); checkerplate steel,
black painted (Number (N)ine)**
CEILING
**bamboo (Soph); checkerplate steel,
black paint (Number (N)ine)**
WINDOW
glass
LIGHTING FIXTURES
Max Ray
SHOWCASE
mirrored stainless steel

PHOTOGRAPHY
Kozo Takayama

NUMBER (N)INE (NAGOYA)

LOCATION
**Ono Building, 1F,
2-22-18 Sakae, Naka-ku,
Nagoya**
CLIENT
Cramp
FLOOR AREA
105 m²
START DESIGN
May 2000
OPENING
September 2000
INTERIOR ARCHITECT
EXIT Metal Work Supply
GENERAL CONSTRUCTOR
IDA
LIGHTING DESIGN
EXIT Metal Work Supply
FLOOR
concrete, black iron plate
WALL
concrete
CEILING
concrete, epoxy paint
WINDOW
glass, iron plate with laser cutting
LIGHTING FIXTURES
Max Ray, surgery lamp (Yamada Shomei)
COUCH BED
steel, vinyl leather
COUNTER
stainless steel, glass

PHOTOGRAPHY
Kozo Takayama

BRAND NEW LAB

LOCATION
**Yokohama Sky Building, 1F,
2-19-12 Takashima, Nishi-ku,
Yokohama**
CLIENT
Durban
FLOOR AREA
210 m²
START DESIGN
November 2000
OPENING
March 2001
INTERIOR ARCHITECT
EXIT Metal Work Supply
GENERAL CONSTRUCTOR
Direc Inc.
LIGHTING DESIGN
EXIT Metal Work Supply
FLOOR
concrete
WALL
plasterboard
CEILING
plasterboard
WINDOW
glass
LIGHTING FIXTURES:
Max Ray
SEATING
EXIT Metal Work Supply
SEATING FABRIC
rough cotton
DISPLAY TABLE
glass, steel
COUNTER
steel

PHOTOGRAPHY
Kozo Takayama

MANO

LOCATION
**RaRa Port Part 1, 2-1-1 Hamacho,
Funabashi-shi, Chiba**
CLIENT
Durban
FLOOR AREA
264 m²
START DESIGN
April 2001
OPENING
1 September 2001
INTERIOR ARCHITECT
EXIT Metal Work Supply
GENERAL CONSTRUCTOR
Direc Inc.
LIGHTING DESIGN
EXIT Metal Work Supply
FLOOR
concrete, thick transparent coating
WALL
concrete, plasterboard
CEILING
skeleton concrete, paint
LIGHTING FIXTURES
Max Ray
CHANDELIER
steel, purple crystal
SEATING
Paul Daly
SEATING FABRIC
vinyl leather
SHOWCASE
glass, steel
COUNTER
steel

PHOTOGRAPHY
Kozo Takayama

EXIT METAL WORK SUPPLY
3-6-5 SHIBA, MINATO-KU, TOKYO, 105-0014 JAPAN
T +81 (0)3-5765-6474 F +81 (0)3-5765-6475
E EXIT@EXIT-MWS.CO.JP

NUMBER (N)INE (EBISU)

A concrete vestibule leading to Number (N)ine's basement outlet in Ebisu features a steel frame at the entrance, a simple logo and a staircase illuminated by pale red light. Enter a narrow door, walk down a dark hall and peer through a cramped opening at what appears to be a triangular space. Dividing the shop in two (lengthwise) is an installation composed of lighting, a railing and an inaccessible catwalk of sorts. A narrow glazed passageway that reminds you to 'keep walking' leads to the cash desk and a second exit that calls itself 'the other side of number (n)ine'. Messages in English emerge at various spots throughout the shop. From a distance, coarse, carelessly striped walls resemble bright, cowhide-printed wallpaper. A plain stainless-steel counter, which doubles as a display case, is a nice contrast to the weather-beaten look of the walls. The same can be said of indirect lighting beneath clothes racks along the wall – a futuristic touch, especially when compared to the shabby surroundings. A raw concrete floor and unfinished ceiling add to the ambience of this hand-me-down hideaway. Relying on the tried-and-true 'cemetery concept' used in other Number (N)ine outlets, EXIT Metal Worksupply pumped this space full of dilapidated design drama. A well-balanced dose of decay is clearly visible, but the gloom of the tomb is less obvious.

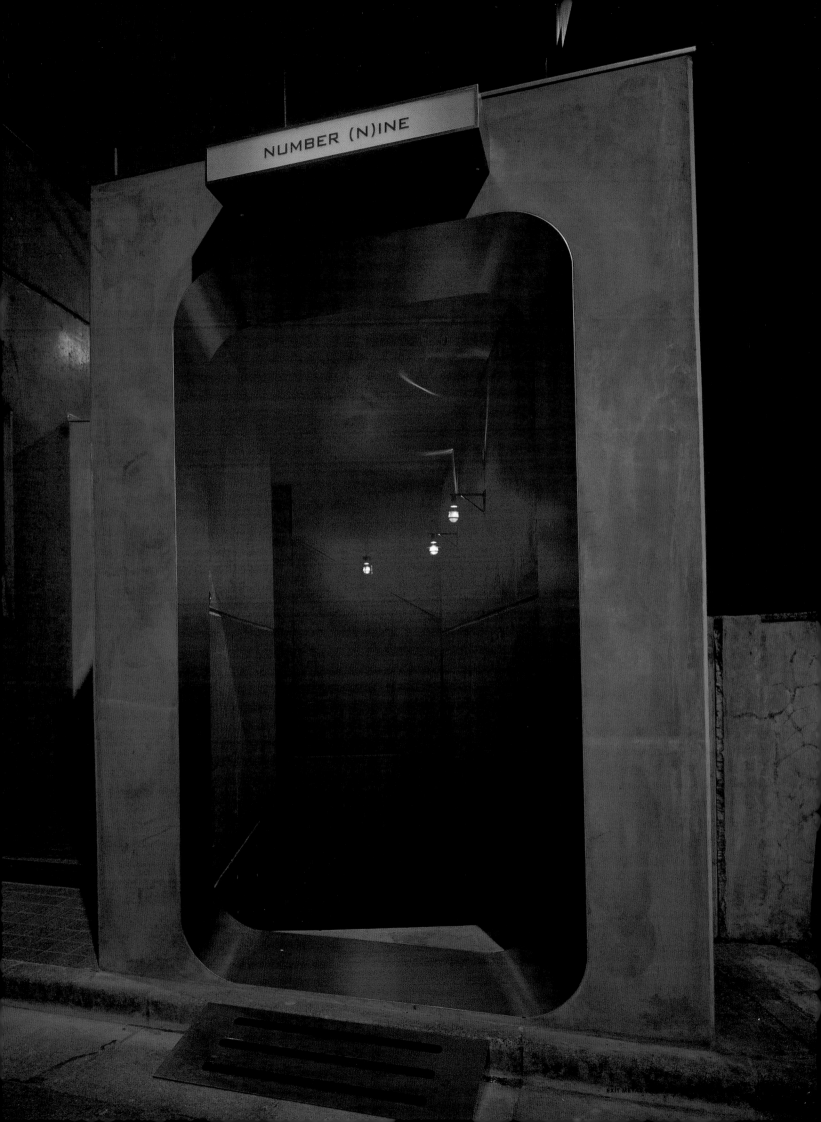

NS MORIOKA

Four long strides and you've passed one of the most remarkable boutiques in the northern city of Morioka without even noticing it. Visible from the street is a long, narrow, cherry-red corridor leading to an ascetically designed shop. Once inside, you might wonder if you're in the right place. Sheets of coal-black metal cover walls and floor. Paint is spattered on the floor, and sliding glass panels on the display cases are broken, giving the impression of work under construction. A closer look reveals an interior the colour of natural bamboo. Narrow to begin with, the space has been coolly sliced in two to create twin shops that go together like night and day, according to the team at EXIT Metal Work Supply. Starting with a basic 'cemetery concept', they added panes of glass that look as though they barely managed to survive a shoot-out in a former life. EXIT had previously used fractured sheets of glass for a fashion show featuring menswear by Number (N)ine. Countless examples shattered to smithereens before these carefully damaged panels were finally in position. The glass panels can also be used as partitions between the two shops. Rounded ceiling sections of bamboo and steel at opposite sides of the space unite the two outlets – Soph and Number (N)ine – creating a coherent whole. Customers visit Soph for business attire and slip across to Number (N)ine to craft a macho-casual image. One for daytime wear, and the other to party deep into the night.

NUMBER (N)INE (NAGOYA)

The rather sombre façade of Nagoya's Number (N)ine has taken a step back from the busy street it faces. The raw exterior effectively shuts out all natural light. Inside, a broad stainless-steel band disappears into the mirror at the rear of the space, giving the shop a semblance of infinity. According to Katsuta, who designs for EXIT Metal Work Supply, the image represents a one-way track running along the coarse concrete floor. The client wanted the space to express the dark, rough reputation of Number (N)ine fashions. As in Morioka, EXIT Metal Work Supply used the eerie atmosphere of a cemetery at night as the point of departure. A black ceiling, dark objects and dim lighting combine to produce the chill of obscurity. Shivering with tension, a wide sofa bed illuminated by a surgical lamp focuses all attention on its sinister potential. Red accents around the fitting rooms and at the bottom of the counter were specifically requested in the brief. A catchy but trite message – TRY AGAIN? – invites customers to visit the cubicles as often as they like. Splashes of colour, words of encouragement and a counter sporting cheerful Jamo lamps (another EXIT design) elevate the otherwise gloomy den to a credible level of friendliness.

BRAND NEW LAB

In a busy shopping area close to Yokohama's harbours, EXIT Metal Work Supply designed a trendy boutique that includes a retro café-restaurant. Diagonal blue lines crisscross the concrete floor. Showcases and four chairs featured at the entrance create a link to the heart of the complex: a café inspired by American-style diners of the '50s. Mat-glass storage units line the walls of the café. Despite the step that separates diner and boutique, a distinction between the two functions is barely noticeable. Characterised by the straightforward placement of its display cases, the narrow shop surrounds the café's seating area. A semitransparent film on the shop windows gives passers-by a blurred view of fashions displayed inside.

Clothes hanging on efficiently mounted rails are clearly illuminated from above, while shoes are presented on trays below. These and other rails throughout the shop have an ultra-minimal look. EXIT Metal Work Supply also designed the showcases and seating elements for this taut, cool interior.

Plain. Simple. Chic.

MANO

Industrial complexes and shopping centres form a continuous urban strip that stretches from Narita International Airport to the heart of Tokyo. Halfway between the two, rising above the drab jumble of buildings is an ugly colossus on stilts: a gargantuan covered ski run. Thanks to the more reasonably priced land here, the shopping centre at the foot of the run boasts roomier shops than those found in downtown Tokyo. Judging by the results, EXIT Metal Work Supply had fun working on the retail project designed for this shopping centre. Hanging prominently at the centre of the shop is a metal curtain, which I saw being welded during my visit to EXIT in the summer of 2001. The interwoven design injects a note of frivolity into the space, although welds left in plain sight give the curtain a rugged look as well. Showcases in various forms and materials are a feast for the eye. Drawers wrapped in transparent acrylic and mounted on metal pipes share the space with ingenious steel installations and no-nonsense rectangular display units. The ambience is both austere and industrial. Three cases are clad in a wood-grained film. The undeniable pièce de résistance, however, is the counter. A display case adorned with lotus blossoms and water lilies afloat on a small pond may not be the most practical of furnishings, but it certainly is pretty. And together with the wooden frame and the projected image of trees directly behind it, the construction gives the space an atmosphere of intimacy. What's more, the counter neatly divides the shop into two zones: one blue, one white. Wooden blinds attractively filter light emanating from light boxes on the blue walls. The concrete floor exhibits a coat of clear varnish. What the designers had in mind was a thicker layer, which would give visitors the impression of walking on water, but the result is not quite what they had envisioned. That's just as well, because this shop really did not need yet another eye-catching element.

FUMITA DESIGN OFFICE
AKIHITO FUMITA

文田 昭仁

While still an art student, Akihito Fumita was more interested in music than in his formal education. 'I played the drums and did quite a bit of composing. That's really how my passion to create got started.' It wasn't until he went to work for a design agency, however, that he realised he was cut out to be a designer.

'I love to take materials intended for one application and use them for something else. A lot of my work is about disregarding an existing relationship between objects and giving that relationship a different form or significance.' A variation on this theme is Fumita's attempt to discover the original meaning of objects or materials, to tinker with what he finds and to come up with a fresh twist. 'The same thing applies to tools,' he says. 'Why should a tool serve only one purpose?' A quick glance at the ceiling, where Fumita has hung several light boxes as uplighters, speaks volumes. In a short time we'll be using identical light boxes to select illustrations for this book.

He has an even more impressive example to show us. Stairs lend access to a meeting room in the basement, but leaving this space is not simply a matter of retracing our steps. A transparent corrugated screen conceals Fumita's files as well as a black builder's hoist threatening DANGER in red letters, our alternative route to the floor above. The apparatus is tucked away between the filing cabinets, and the lack of a lift shaft creates a kind of window that looks out on the ground floor and the glass façade of the premises. Daylight penetrates the underground space through this opening.

Fumita recalls how difficult it was in the early years to make a correct estimate of the budget needed for a particular project. 'Nothing is more frustrating than having to choose a material on the basis of price rather than quality,' he says. Even so, a good design is more than a matter of financing. 'Japan's bubble economy [prosperous period in the late 1980s] practically made money grow on trees, but did it result in better design?' he wonders. 'Fortunately, the kind of extravagant projects realised during those years are a thing of the past. Designers today are forced to be inventive in their use of materials, and more often than not

the outcome is refreshing. A limited budget doesn't necessarily stop you from making interesting things.'

Having turned the conversation back to materials, Fumita is off and running. Working on a Nissan project, for example, he created an alternating stream of filtered light with a perforated foam plastic normally used for insulation. He comes up with remarkable effects simply by coating standard materials like OSB (Oriented Strand Board). He's equally enthusiastic about metal, particularly steel – 'easy to use, gives you loads of freedom' – as well as various types of plastic, although many of them 'aren't cheap'. And artificial marble, he remarks, is another standard product that can assume different guises. The list is endless.

In addition to materials, the designer likes to experiment with light. The Nissan project is one case in point. Another is Fumita's work on retail outlets for Natural Body, where indirect lighting obscures corners and, consequently, makes it hard for observers to gauge the dimensions of a shop. The space seems to have no beginning and no end.

Fumita's approach to a project is to become thoroughly familiar with what the client wants, to develop a concept and to reduce it to its simplest form. Contributing factors such as time, cost, product, service and available space have a direct influence, of course, on design, materials and implementation. 'In shop design, my main concern is restraint. The design is simply a means of displaying the merchandise. That's my top priority.'

Those whose work he admires, says the man with goatee, gleaming pate and pint-size glasses, include Shiro Kuramata, whom he believes has 'probably influenced everyone in Japan'. As a student, he also looked to architect Arata Isozaki for inspiration. 'After reading several books about him, I became fascinated by his architectonic language.' Asked if certain products stimulate his creativity, Fumita admits to finding cars a remarkable turn on. It's no big surprise to hear that a guy dressed from head to toe in black also drives a black Audi TT. 'If you stop to think about what makes a car a car – technology,

'IN SHOP DESIGN, MY MAIN CONCERN IS RESTRAINT. THE DESIGN IS SIMPLY A MEANS OF DISPLAYING THE MERCHANDISE'

power, safety and design – you have to agree it's an incredible product. Exceptionally high quality for a reasonable price. It's got almost everything.'

Fumita's work demonstrates a dual fascination with the future and the abstract. More than one of his designs suggest the interior of a spaceship. He shapes an otherworldly ambience by stripping a space of all familiar connotations. Fumita believes that even though an object may seem to convey a straightforward message, there's always a discrepancy between the visual image and its verbal expression. He uses this concept to reach a level of abstraction – a place in the future, as it were – which allows the design to be interpreted in any number of ways. The concealed corners and recessed lighting that mark his designs for Natural Body and Nissan, respectively, represent Fumita's attempt to eliminate a horizon line and thus move his work into the realm of abstraction.

The Nissan project moved him in another direction as well. It was his first experience with a commercial space focused on service: a retail space based not only on selling a product but also on providing information. Rather than highlighting the service aspect, however, he opted for a clean environment that appears strangely indifferent to the human presence. Instead he used futuristic monitors à la *Mission Impossible* to emphasise the role that technology plays at Nissan.

Fumita toys with the thought of designing other service-oriented establishments, including hotels and banks. 'So many of today's banks project a cheap image. It won't be long before everybody's banking online, which means fewer financial institutions in the city. Those still operating in the future will have to make a more distinctive impression. After all, a bank is where you put your money. It's an eminent organisation. Producing the quality essential to that image and filling the space with invisible bank-related functions is an exciting idea.'

The multifaceted designer winds up the conversation by comparing Japan with the United States. Fumita finds people in his country more conscious of the importance of retail design. 'Americans make a clear distinction between "design" and "no design",' he says. He can't imagine a huge American-style, self-service store making a splash in Japan. 'Fortunately for me, the Japanese aren't comfortable without at least a smattering of design.'

FUMITA DESIGN OFFICE
AKIHITO FUMITA

文田 昭仁

TRE PINI

LOCATION
5-2-3 Koujidai, Nishi-ku, Kobe-shi,
Hyogo
CLIENT
Oggi International
FLOOR AREA
55 m²
START DESIGN
January 1998
OPENING
March 1998
INTERIOR ARCHITECT
Akihito Fumita
GENERAL CONSTRUCTOR
Daiwa Kogyo
LIGHTING DESIGN
Max Ray
FLOOR
oriented strand board, clear polyurethane
paint finish
WALL
plasterboard, epoxy resin
LOUVER
oriented strand board, clear tint finish
CEILING
plasterboard
LIGHTING FIXTURES
Ushio Spax
COUNTER/TABLE
oriented strand board, clear tint finish
SHOWCASE
oriented strand board, glass

PHOTOGRAPHY
Nacása & Partners

TICTAC

LOCATION
Shibuya Parco, 1F,
14-5 Utagawacho, Shibuya-ku,
Tokyo
CLIENT
A-Cross
FLOOR AREA
39 m²
START DESIGN
August 1999
OPENING
October 1999
INTERIOR ARCHITECT
Akihito Fumita
GENERAL CONSTRUCTOR
Parco Promotions
LIGHTING DESIGN
Ushio Spax
FLOOR
oriented strand board, clear polyurethane
paint finish
WALL
plasterboard, epoxy resin
CEILING
plasterboard, epoxy resin
LIGHTING FIXTURES
Ushio Spax
COUNTER
oriented strand board
SHOWCASE
clear glass, steel

PHOTOGRAPHY
Nacása & Partners

NATURAL BODY

LOCATION
Hankyu International, 1F,
19-19 Chayamachi, Kita-ku,
Osaka
CLIENT
Natural Body
FLOOR AREA
109 m²
START DESIGN
September 2000
OPENING
November 2000
INTERIOR ARCHITECT
Akihito Fumita
GENERAL CONSTRUCTOR
Kan Associates
LIGHTING DESIGN
Max Ray
FLOOR
off-white vinyl tile
WALL
plasterboard, epoxy resin in stripe pattern
(mat and gloss)
CEILING
plasterboard, epoxy resin in stripe pattern
(mat and gloss), steel
WINDOW
glass
LIGHTING FIXTURES
Max Ray
SEATING
Fumita Design Office
SEATING FABRIC
leather
COUNTER
lacquered wood, stainless steel
SHOWCASE
steel, acrylic

PHOTOGRAPHY
Nacása & Partners

NISSAN GINZA GALLERY

LOCATION
5-8-1 Ginza, Chuo-ku,
Tokyo
CLIENT
Nissan
FLOOR AREA
360 m², including 68 m² backyard
START DESIGN
October 2000
OPENING
18 June 2001
ARCHITECT
Akihito Fumita
INTERIOR ARCHITECT
Akihito Fumita
PRODUCTION
Hakuhodo Inc.
VISUAL SOUND SYSTEM
International Creative Co.
LIGHTING DESIGN
Ushio Spax
GENERAL CONSTRUCTOR
Taisei Corporation (exterior);
D.Brain Co. (interior)
FLOOR
embossed stainless steel tile (first floor);
porcelain tile by Inax (entrance hall,
second floor)
WALL
aluminium rib-louver (exterior); embossed
PVC panel by Idée (entrance hall);
aluminium rib louver, acrylic artificial
marble (entrance hall, second floor)
FAÇADE SIGN
stainless steel
CEILING
glass wool, acrylic enamel paint finish (first
floor); punching stainless steel panel
(entrance hall); plasterboard, acrylic
emergent paint (entrance hall, second floor)
WINDOW
stainless steel sashes
LIGHTING FIXTURES
Ushio Spax
ACCESSORIES
stainless steel concierge counter,
web kiosk, info shower and water server
RECEPTION COUNTER
acrylic artificial marble
(Korylite KL-1 by Advan)
STOOL
stainless steel, synthetic leather
BENCH
stainless steel, synthetic leather

PHOTOGRAPHY
Nacása & Partners

FUMITA DESIGN OFFICE
FUMITA DESIGN OFFICE
FUMITA DESIGN OFFICE
FUMITA DESIGN OFFICE
FUMITA DESIGN OFFICE
FUMITA DESIGN OFFICE
FUMITA DESIGN OFFICE
FUMITA DESIGN OFFICE
FUMITA DESIGN OFFICE
FUMITA DESIGN OFFICE
FUMITA DESIGN OFFICE
FUMITA DESIGN OFFICE
FUMITA DESIGN OFFICE
FUMITA DESIGN OFFICE
FUMITA DESIGN OFFICE
FUMITA DESIGN OFFICE
FUMITA DESIGN OFFICE
FUMITA DESIGN OFFICE
FUMITA DESIGN OFFICE
FUMITA DESIGN OFFICE
FUMITA DESIGN OFFICE
FUMITA DESIGN OFFICE
FUMITA DESIGN OFFICE
FUMITA DESIGN OFFICE
FUMITA DESIGN OFFICE
FUMITA DESIGN OFFICE
FUMITA DESIGN OFFICE
FUMITA DESIGN OFFICE
FUMITA DESIGN OFFICE
FUMITA DESIGN OFFICE
FUMITA DESIGN OFFICE
FUMITA DESIGN OFFICE
FUMITA DESIGN OFFICE
FUMITA DESIGN OFFICE
FUMITA DESIGN OFFICE
FUMITA DESIGN OFFICE
FUMITA DESIGN OFFICE
FUMITA DESIGN OFFICE
FUMITA DESIGN OFFICE
FUMITA DESIGN OFFICE
FUMITA DESIGN OFFICE
FUMITA DESIGN OFFICE
FUMITA DESIGN OFFICE
FUMITA DESIGN OFFICE
FUMITA DESIGN OFFICE
FUMITA DESIGN OFFICE
FUMITA DESIGN OFFICE
FUMITA DESIGN OFFICE
FUMITA DESIGN OFFICE
FUMITA DESIGN OFFICE
FUMITA DESIGN OFFICE
FUMITA DESIGN OFFICE
FUMITA DESIGN OFFICE
FUMITA DESIGN OFFICE
FUMITA DESIGN OFFICE
FUMITA DESIGN OFFICE
FUMITA DESIGN OFFICE
FUMITA DESIGN OFFICE
FUMITA DESIGN OFFICE
FUMITA DESIGN OFFICE
FUMITA DESIGN OFFICE

FUMITA DESIGN OFFICE
FUKUDA BLDG. 1+B1F, 2-18-2 MINAMI AOYAMA, MINATO-KU, TOKYO, 107-0062 JAPAN
T +81 (0)3-5414-2880 F +81 (0)3-5414-2881
E FDESIGN@TKY3.3WEB.NE.JP

TRE PINI

The client wanted to use this space – located in a shopping centre on the outskirts of Kobe – not only for retail purposes but also as a room for cultural gatherings. With a target group in mind of women between 30 and 50 – a category known in Japan as 'the older housewife' – Akihito Fumita decided to create a space filled with warm colours and subdued lighting. He used a kind of fibreboard for the floor, as well as for nearly all display surfaces, from tables and counters to wall-mounted shelves. Highlighting the shop is an elaborately designed display wall. Light filters into the space through wooden blinds, creating a pattern that accentuates round acrylic display units containing accessories. Panels installed at a slight angle rise in a sweeping flow to become part of the sloping ceiling.

When lighting is dim, the ambience is almost mysterious. To keep the premises multifunctional, Fumita used the periphery of the room for displaying merchandise and left the central area more or less empty. A solitary table can be reduced in size or moved to the side of the room. Bearing the name Tre Pini, a large square panel on the exterior of the shop turns out to be a sliding door. When events are being held, this door partly closes off the entrance without blocking the view of the space. Simple but effective.

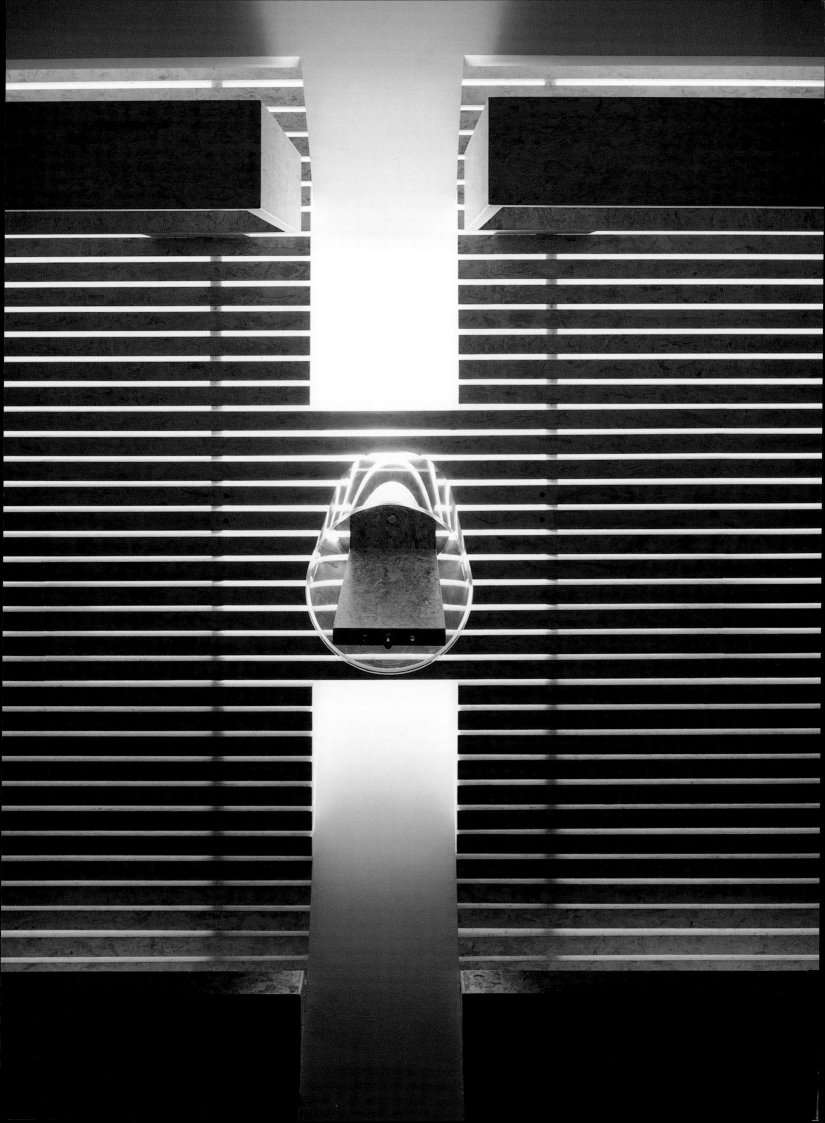

TICTAC

This compact watch shop is located in a department store in Shibuya, a Tokyo district favoured by the city's youth. Akihito Fumita approached the TicTac project as if it were a graphic design. Tucked rhythmically into the walls are cylindrical showcases of various sizes. A glass-clad counter is the only object that touches the floor without first making a detour. Fumita installed a hanging partition that creates extra room for displaying merchandise while also separating the shop from the department store proper. The contrast between TicTac's black exterior and the pure white space inside is softened by flooring and counter components of fibreboard panelling, which add a casual note to the interior. A clever recess in a corner of the counter houses four trays that appear like magic when required. The transparent acrylic display cases are attractive, but not particularly practical. To access the merchandise, the cylindrical cases have to be unlocked and revolved until a slit appears. Unfortunately, the cylinder doesn't remain in the open position unless held steady. Consequently, the salesperson has to wrestle with both key and slit while attempting to retrieve the contents and serve the waiting customer. A flaw in an otherwise beautifully designed interior.

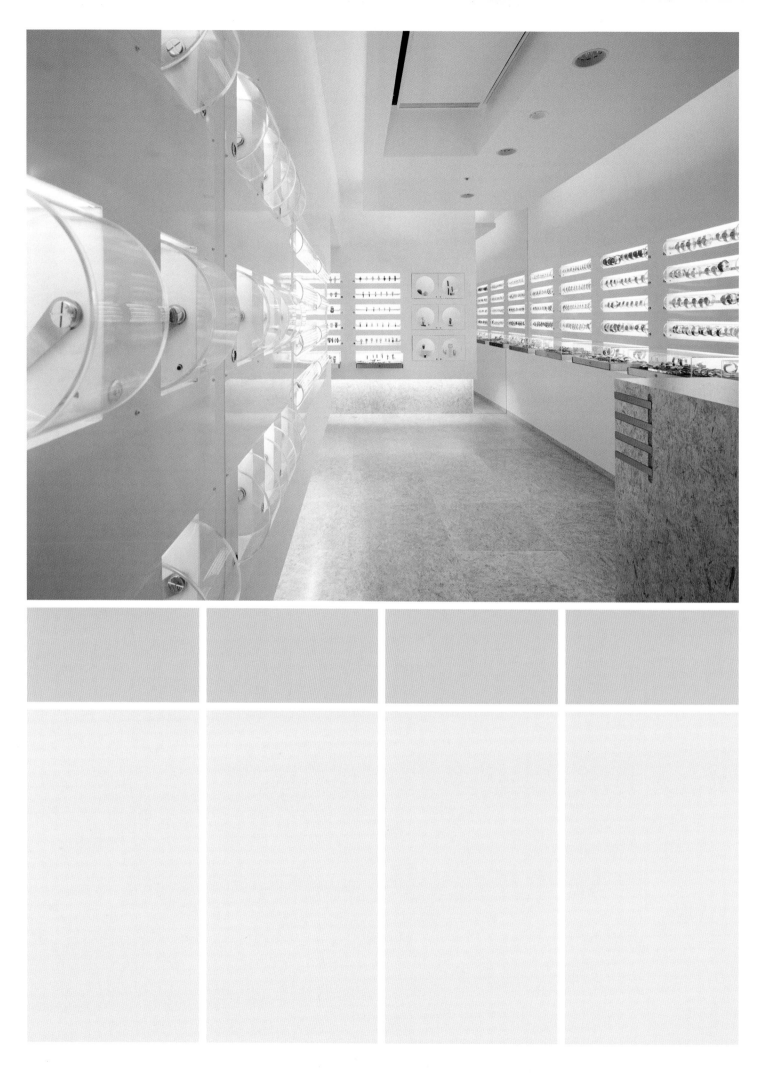

NATURAL BODY

The founder of Natural Body envisioned a chain of massage salons that would appeal to the customers of trendy boutiques. According to the company slogan, 'Outer beauty begins only after inner beauty and relaxation are achieved.' Natural Body outlets are often located, therefore, in the fashion sections of major department stores. Called in to design these salons, Akihito Fumita was asked to create a fresh, serene space complete with ergonomic furniture: an entity that would truly contribute to a peaceful state of mind. The abstract shapes of massage tables and chairs are a feast for the eye. Taking care to conceal the metal frames, Fumita designed three different pieces of furniture for three types of massage: one for back and shoulders, one for feet and one for the body as a whole. No complicated high-tech devices, but convenient objects with futuristic shapes and amusing features, such as an opening to accommodate the nose. Huge 'ears' on the foot-massage chair shield the customer from unwanted glances, thus providing an additional degree of privacy without taking up any extra space.

In the Hankyu International Hotel in Osaka, the entrance to Natural Body is hidden away on the north side of the building. A display unit holding dozens of bottles of mineral water grabs the eye of the passer-by and leads it away from the massage tables. Inside, broad horizontal blinds completely screen off the commotion of a taxi rank along the kerb. Only the trees across the street are visible. Horizontal stripes of mat and gloss paint add a touch of relief to the walls.

In his designs for Natural Body, Fumita plays with an awareness of time and space. Thanks to an ingenious indirect-lighting system and to undulating patterns on walls and ceiling, the space has no obvious demarcations.

The paradoxical result is both intimate and futuristic.

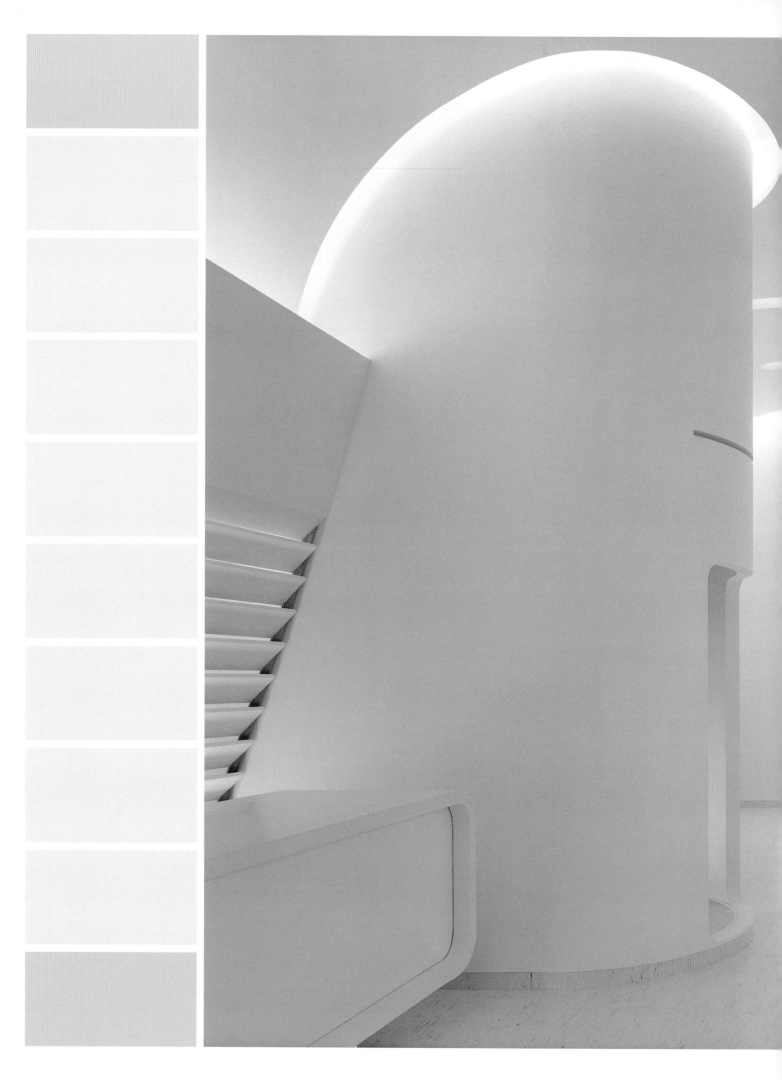

NISSAN GINZA GALLERY

Located on a bustling corner of Ginza's main intersection, the renovated Nissan gallery injects a subdued note of freshness into the luxurious commercial heart of Tokyo. Surrounded by exclusive department stores and the glare of neon signs, the two-storey white façade with its single Nissan logo is a welcome breath of simplicity. Step inside, however, and the illusion turns into a good imitation of a sci-fi movie set. Monitors displaying a wealth of Nissan-related information look like tantalising instruments for sending a spaceship to Mars, and the corrugated-steel showroom almost tingles with otherworldly vibrations. Akihito Fumita shaped this futuristic atmosphere with his creative use of materials. He manipulated a basically plain design by introducing all sorts of relief into his materials. Nissan's two latest models greet visitors to the showroom with a visual explosion. The gigantic, cleverly illuminated box lined in corrugated, stainless-steel panels has a macho look. The floor glistens with dozens of built-in spots, which are complemented by an array of identical lights recessed into the ceiling. Canary-yellow sofas with fanciful cubist lines are built low to the ground to make the space look even larger. Daylight enters from large windows on three sides of the room. Projecting from the information area above is a fourth window. Fumita created two bright white rooms with indirect lighting for product information and all related services. Light passing through gridded panels of artificial marble illuminates these spaces. The trip upstairs – two disorienting revolutions around a spiral staircase – seems endless. The compact white room at the top of the stairs houses an island of suspended monitors provided with high stools. Here the visitor can look down at the showroom through a 1-metre-wide window framed in stainless steel.

近藤 康夫

A huge bottle of Laurent Perrier gathers dust at a corner of the stairway in Yasuo Kondo's office. It's a souvenir of the festivities that surrounded what Kondo acknowledges is his biggest and best project of the past 20 years. Earlier this year he received the prestigious Mainichi Design Award 2000 for his renovation of the Tokyo Stock Exchange. The soft-spoken man in his early fifties discusses the project with the same nonchalance and modesty that characterise everything he says about his work.

Kondo (1950) claims that his being a designer has more to do with coincidence than with determination. 'I really wanted to be a teacher,' he says. 'I was thinking of a field like social studies or perhaps sociology. But another subject offered at the university was art, and the idea of art education appealed to me as well. My previous studies had nothing at all to do with art, so I entered the art academy. I began by selecting architecture, more or less at random, and before I knew it I was taking courses in graphic and product design.' He grins at the memory. 'It took about two years before all the pieces started coming together in my mind. Around that time I also became interested in Italian lamps, which displayed a variety of incredible forms. The impression that these objects and others made on me awakened a faint flair for design, but I'm basically a man without talent,' says he whose typical Japanese understatement is quashed by designs that capture one prize after another.

Following graduation, Kondo spent four years at Masahiro Miwa Architects before joining his great role model and mentor Shiro Kuramata to concentrate on interior and product design. 'Kuramata was a genius,' he declares. 'His whole life revolved around design, although he was not out to create something timeless. His designs came to him quite naturally. Kuramata worked on virtually every design-related front. He was complete.' Kuramata influenced Kondo's view of interior design. 'I see interior design as a mathematical equation,' he says. 'Architecture involves a great deal of theorisation on the subject of space, but the same kind of analysis is rarely found in interior design.' In 1989 Kondo made his own contribution to the cause in the form of a bilingual

book, *Interior Space Designing*, in which he explains his manner of working in a straightforward, systematic way.

In analysing his own work, Kondo distinguishes three phases of activity. 'First of all, it's important to envision a space as if it were empty,' he says. 'I like to strip it down to the skeleton before taking a look at the construction. The challenge lies in reorganising the space.' He pauses to marshal his thoughts. 'When you're in a space, what you actually have is a space within a space. The volume that you see differs from the real volume.' In Kondo's mind, every space is a dual entity.

In the second phase, he observes the space three-dimensionally, as a cube. It's this interpretation of the space that he combines with the wishes of his client. 'It's very systematic,' he says, rapidly sketching as he speaks. 'A child could do it.' After a moment of deliberation, however, he looks up and admits that quite often it's not that simple. 'Of course, there are other things to be considered, such as materials, colours and forms. But these are not pressing matters,' he says calmly before pointing out the inevitable limitation: 'I'm not very good at designing big stores. Simply increasing the scale doesn't work. The sense of space in a large project is highly complex. Such projects are akin to architecture, and I'm utterly fascinated by the point at which interior design communes with architecture.'

The third and final phase of his work deals with form and, to a lesser extent, colour and material. 'For a long time I thought it was essential to use extraordinary and outrageous shapes, but the forms I'm creating at the moment are more comprehensible.' Colour plays only a minor role in Kondo's work. Although he's used red as a contrast in several projects, he chose the colour because 'it has few gradations and is fairly unambiguous'. Nowadays Kondo opts for quieter colours, forms and materials. 'I want the overall image to be pleasant, not garish.'

He's not at all interested in discussing style. 'Nor do I approach a project with certain images in my head, like other designers I've heard about, who allegedly envision a deep blue sea, perhaps, or an ancient city. People may find my methods strange, but they

hold no mystery for me.' Again he insists that a lack of talent has made it necessary for him to rely on logic. 'I work with a basic pattern,' he explains. 'Nearly 90 per cent of a design is determined by the preliminary plan. It's playing with the surface area of a space that provides all the fun.'

An overview of Kondo's oeuvre has to begin with his first independent project and undeniably his greatest challenge, a 1981 exhibition design for Comme des Garçons. 'The nerve-racking desire to do a good job is something I'll never forget.' The exhibition catapulted him into the higher echelons of interior design. Entitled *Robe de Chambre*, the show guided visitors through a distinctive labyrinth of totally different spaces.

Although known for his work in retail design, Kondo has an even greater reputation in the world of business-related projects. He sees the offices of Polygon Pictures – where he used colourful accents to expose the structure of the building – as a breakthrough in this area of his work. And when the subject is his pièce de résistance, the Tokyo Stock Exchange, he cannot conceal a satisfied smile of restrained pride. Not for nothing is he referred to as 'the figurehead of modern Japanese interior design'. Backing this appellation is a long list of projects featuring bold forms and a beautifully severe functionality.

Contemplating the future, the designer thinks of doing the interior of a museum or renovating a historical building. The latter is not as easy as it may seem in a country with so few old buildings. 'As a designer,' he says, 'I have to consider the added value attached to everything I make. A space must have a function. Being cool or trendy is not enough. The Japanese often differentiate between function and design. A good example is the design of our museums, which leaves much room for improvement.' Kondo recognises an obvious similarity between museums and boutiques. 'In both cases, people come not for the interior but for the contents of the interior. The surrounding space must do no more than provide a backdrop for the objects it contains.'

The Japanese fascination with shopping amazes the designer. 'I see no clear-cut line of thinking in all this frenzy to buy. When I walk the dog, I find ugliness everywhere I look.' He shakes his head. 'Someone living in a tiny, unsightly dwelling has an expensive Mercedes Benz protruding from his garage. People combine catchpenny items of clothing with designer outfits. Totally out of balance and ugly as sin. We're into crossbreeding in this country. It's all about status symbols, which the Japanese mix up in the weirdest ways.'

Kondo refuses to participate in the madness. Not a big spender, he puts his hard-earned money in his pocket. Neither he nor his wife has a driving licence. He's not ostentatious. His office looks almost uninhabited. The rather dated exterior of the building is clad in wavy white perforated panelling similar to that used in a retail project for Yohji Yamamoto, a job that featured these and other industrial remnants. His private office on the third floor is orderly and spacious, but other rooms are filled with computers, papers, maquettes and books. Here and there a trophy testifying to his success casts a nonchalant eye at the clutter. Finding time to properly display awards is not a Kondo priority.

YASUO KONDO DESIGN OFFICE
YASUO KONDO

近藤 康夫

CASSINA INTER DÉCOR

LOCATION
2-12-14 Minami-Aoyama, Minato-ku,
Tokyo
CLIENT
Cassina Inter Décor Japan
FLOOR AREA
2007 m²
START DESIGN
June 1997 (third floor: January 2000)
OPENING
December 1997 (third floor: June 2000)
INTERIOR ARCHITECT
Yasuo Kondo
GENERAL CONSTRUCTOR
TKO (first, second floor); Biruto (third floor)
LIGHTING DESIGN
Yasuo Kondo (first, second floor);
Masanobu Takeishi (ICE) (third floor)
FLOOR
glass, white ash wood, limestone (first,
second floor); aluminium, elm wood (third
floor)
WALL
glass (first, second floor); plasterboard,
painted melapi wood, glass, aluminium,
screens (Fractal) (third floor)
CEILING
plasterboard; glass (second floor)
LIGHTING FIXTURES
Endo (first, second floor); Modular Japan
(second, third floor)
SHOWCASES
glass

PHOTOGRAPHY
Nacása & Partners

YOHJI YAMAMOTO / YOHJI YAMAMOTO (HOMME) / YOHJI YAMAMOTO + NOIR

LOCATION
Kobe Bal, 6F,
3-6-1 Sannomiya-cho, Chuo-ku,
Kobe
CLIENT
Yohji Yamamoto
FLOOR AREA
120 m²
START DESIGN
June 1998
OPENING
September 1998
INTERIOR ARCHITECT
Yasuo Kondo
GENERAL CONSTRUCTOR
Make Design Office
LIGHTING DESIGN
Yasuo Kondo
FLOOR
steel plate
WALL
steelplate
CEILING
plasterboard
WINDOW
glass, blinds
ACCESSORIES
antique door
SHELVING
3.2-mm steel plate

PHOTOGRAPHY
Nacása & Partners

YOHJI YAMAMOTO (KYOTO)

LOCATION
Kyoto Bal, 2F,
3-Jyo Sagaru, Kawaramachi dori,
Nakagyo-ku, Kyoto
CLIENT
Yohji Yamamoto
FLOOR AREA
82 m²
START DESIGN
December 1998
OPENING
19 February 1999
INTERIOR ARCHITECT
Yasuo Kondo
GENERAL CONSTRUCTOR
Make Design Office
LIGHTING DESIGN
Yasuo Kondo
FLOOR
steel plate
WALL
steel plate
CEILING
plasterboard
SHELVING
3.2-mm steel plate

PHOTOGRAPHY
Nacása & Partners

YOHJI YAMAMOTO (HOMME) / Y'S FOR MEN RED LABEL (TOKYO)

LOCATION
Matsuya Ginza, 5F,
3-6-1, Ginza, Chuo-ku,
Tokyo
CLIENT
Yohji Yamamoto
FLOOR AREA
98 m²
START DESIGN
June 2000
OPENING
30 September 2000
INTERIOR ARCHITECT
Yasuo Kondo
GENERAL CONSTRUCTOR
Build Co.
LIGHTING DESIGN
Yasuo Kondo
FLOOR
steel plate
WALL
steel plate
CEILING
plasterboard
SHELVING
3.2-mm steel plate

PHOTOGRAPHY
Nacása & Partners

YOHJI YAMAMOTO + NOIR (OSAKA)

LOCATION
Kintetsu Abeno, 4F,
1-1-43 Abenosuji, Abeno-ku,
Osaka
CLIENT
Yohji Yamamoto
FLOOR AREA
46 m²
START DESIGN
January 2001
OPENING
22 March 2001
INTERIOR ARCHITECT
Yasuo Kondo
GENERAL CONSTRUCTOR
Nomura Kogei
LIGHTING DESIGN
Yasuo Kondo
FLOOR
aluminium
WALL
aluminium, copper
CEILING
plasterboard
SHELVING
aluminium, copper

PHOTOGRAPHY
Nacása & Partners

YASUO KONDO DESIGN OFFICE
YASUO KONDO DESIGN OFFICE
YASUO KONDO DESIGN OFFICE
YASUO KONDO DESIGN OFFICE
YASUO KONDO DESIGN OFFICE
YASUO KONDO DESIGN OFFICE
YASUO KONDO DESIGN OFFICE
YASUO KONDO DESIGN OFFICE
YASUO KONDO DESIGN OFFICE
YASUO KONDO DESIGN OFFICE
YASUO KONDO DESIGN OFFICE
YASUO KONDO DESIGN OFFICE
YASUO KONDO DESIGN OFFICE
YASUO KONDO DESIGN OFFICE
YASUO KONDO DESIGN OFFICE
YASUO KONDO DESIGN OFFICE
YASUO KONDO DESIGN OFFICE
YASUO KONDO DESIGN OFFICE
YASUO KONDO DESIGN OFFICE
YASUO KONDO DESIGN OFFICE
YASUO KONDO DESIGN OFFICE
YASUO KONDO DESIGN OFFICE
YASUO KONDO DESIGN OFFICE
YASUO KONDO DESIGN OFFICE
YASUO KONDO DESIGN OFFICE
YASUO KONDO DESIGN OFFICE
YASUO KONDO DESIGN OFFICE
YASUO KONDO DESIGN OFFICE
YASUO KONDO DESIGN OFFICE
YASUO KONDO DESIGN OFFICE
YASUO KONDO DESIGN OFFICE
YASUO KONDO DESIGN OFFICE
YASUO KONDO DESIGN OFFICE
YASUO KONDO DESIGN OFFICE
YASUO KONDO DESIGN OFFICE
YASUO KONDO DESIGN OFFICE
YASUO KONDO DESIGN OFFICE
YASUO KONDO DESIGN OFFICE
YASUO KONDO DESIGN OFFICE
YASUO KONDO DESIGN OFFICE
YASUO KONDO DESIGN OFFICE
YASUO KONDO DESIGN OFFICE
YASUO KONDO DESIGN OFFICE
YASUO KONDO DESIGN OFFICE
YASUO KONDO DESIGN OFFICE
YASUO KONDO DESIGN OFFICE
YASUO KONDO DESIGN OFFICE
YASUO KONDO DESIGN OFFICE
YASUO KONDO DESIGN OFFICE
YASUO KONDO DESIGN OFFICE
YASUO KONDO DESIGN OFFICE
YASUO KONDO DESIGN OFFICE
YASUO KONDO DESIGN OFFICE
YASUO KONDO DESIGN OFFICE
YASUO KONDO DESIGN OFFICE
YASUO KONDO DESIGN OFFICE
YASUO KONDO DESIGN OFFICE
YASUO KONDO DESIGN OFFICE

YASUO KONDO DESIGN OFFICE
3-24-24 NISHI-AZABU, MINATO-KU, TOKYO, 106-0031 JAPAN
T +81 (0)3-3408-0981 F +81 (0)3-3408-0983
E OFFICE@KON-DO.CO.JP

CASSINA INTER DÉCOR

The client, who produced meticulous
plans for the design of Cassina Inter
Décor, asked for an unadorned,
contemporary look with a hint of the
Orient. Yasuo Kondo responded by
dividing the interior of this furniture
store into various semi-open spaces
featuring several striking installations.
At ground level, where home accessories
are located, a surprising structure of
white metal cubes with built-in lighting
provides an exclusive spot for each
accessory displayed. A broad illuminated
stairway – reminiscent of Hollywood
musicals – leads to a rather cosy corner
of the shop. Upstairs, a 30-metre-long
half-round illuminated wall that curves
over the display counters takes centre
stage. This eye-catcher gathers the
kaleidoscope of moods that permeate
the store and fuses them into a logical
entity. Kondo designed the shop
to accommodate a diversity of styles.
Japanese elements on the top floor
include sliding wood panels introduced
for flexibility. The use of wood, along
with chunky pebbles and mat-glass
panels, gives the otherwise ultramodern,
pared-down space an unexpected
whisper of warmth. On this floor another
installation – a large, snow-white cube –
doubles as the shop's art gallery.
Thanks to Kondo's concept, a visit
to Cassina Inter Décor becomes a brief
but well-organised voyage of discovery.

YOHJI YAMAMOTO / YOHJI YAMAMOTO (HOMME) / YOHJI YAMAMOTO + NOIR

In most retail spaces, different materials are used to express different dimensions. The first time Yasuo Kondo designed a shop for Yohji Yamamoto, however, he opted for a minimum of materials. With a continuous, uniform image in mind, he conjured up a space made almost completely of steel. Display cases resembling ribbons rise from the floor. Painted white inside and positioned lengthwise, they accentuate the long, narrow form of the shop. The coolly austere interior is a perfect backdrop for Yohji Yamamoto's fashions, many of which are black and virtually all of which are clearly identifiable by their arty asymmetric and utterly simple designs. Totally incongruous is the antique door that functions as a so-called 'entrance' – a humorous accent injected by Yamamoto himself.

YOHJI YAMAMOTO (KYOTO)

Following his initial project for Yohji Yamamoto – a shop with a homogeneous metallic look in which showcases rise like ribbons from the floor – Yasuo Kondo decided to provide the next Yamamoto outlet with a spectacular object that would dominate the entire space. His aim was to focus all attention on Yamamoto's fashions.

Kondo emphasised the big carousel at the centre of the shop by adding floor lighting, which radiates from the core of the cylindrical showcase.

Slender shelves ascending in the manner of a spiral staircase are an ingenious example of craftsmanship. One almost expects an encouraging nudge to set the carousel in motion. The colossal object makes quite an impression amidst the conventional shops-in-a-shop that set the tone in this trendy department store. White walls, white ceiling and a steel-clad floor give the room a frosty ambience. Yamamoto's minimalist ready-to-wear collection comes to the fore in this simple but stylish interior.

YOHJI YAMAMOTO HOMME / Y'S FOR MEN RED LABEL (TOKYO)

In designing his eighth shop for Yohji Yamamoto, Yasuo Kondo created an interior based primarily on rounded shapes. The appearance of the boutique relies on two elements that look as though they are draped around columns. A butterfly-like showcase of glass with a metal top surrounds one angular column. Inside, two monitors present images of Yamamoto's latest fashion show. Two protruding sections of this storage and display unit, which extends approximately 6 metres into the space, contain accessories. The column lends access to the display cases. Encircling the other column is an almost swirling elliptical volume featuring shelves. Both installations invite the visitor to view them from all angles and, in so doing, to explore the entire shop. At the back of the space, metal floor panels continue up the wall in a flowing line. The rail projecting from this surface holds fashions that seem to float in air. The counter and a white side wall are antidotes to stuffiness. Dim lighting and mat-grey objects produce an atmosphere tinged with enough mystery to sweep you away, at least mentally, from the fifth floor of a bustling Tokyo department store.

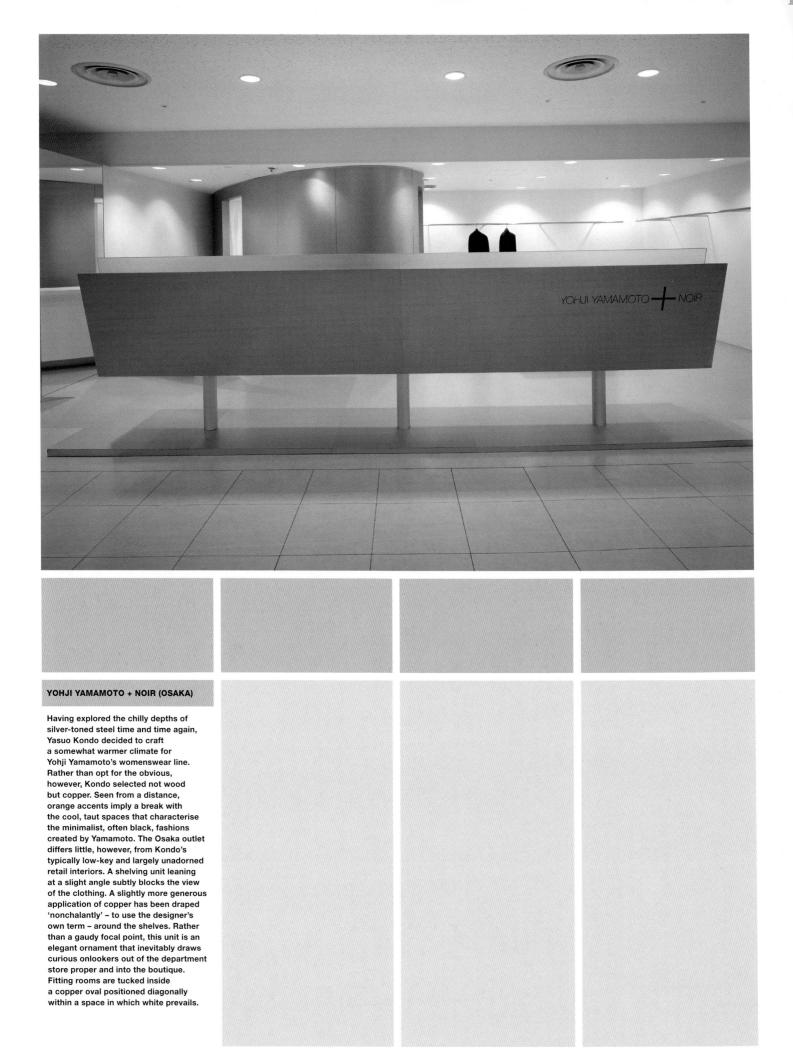

YOHJI YAMAMOTO + NOIR (OSAKA)

Having explored the chilly depths of
silver-toned steel time and time again,
Yasuo Kondo decided to craft
a somewhat warmer climate for
Yohji Yamamoto's womenswear line.
Rather than opt for the obvious,
however, Kondo selected not wood
but copper. Seen from a distance,
orange accents imply a break with
the cool, taut spaces that characterise
the minimalist, often black, fashions
created by Yamamoto. The Osaka outlet
differs little, however, from Kondo's
typically low-key and largely unadorned
retail interiors. A shelving unit leaning
at a slight angle subtly blocks the view
of the clothing. A slightly more generous
application of copper has been draped
'nonchalantly' – to use the designer's
own term – around the shelves. Rather
than a gaudy focal point, this unit is an
elegant ornament that inevitably draws
curious onlookers out of the department
store proper and into the boutique.
Fitting rooms are tucked inside
a copper oval positioned diagonally
within a space in which white prevails.

YOHJI YAMAMOTO + NOIR

黒川 勉

Chuckling as he recalls the opposition of his parents and teachers to the announcement that he wanted to study design, Tsutomu Kurokawa says that in the rural prefecture of Aichi, where he grew up, the idea came as somewhat of a surprise. 'I've always loved beautiful designs, especially cars, fashions and graphics. But no one took my talent seriously, so it was off to the polytechnic to learn about the inner workings of cars.' After a year as a mechanic for a Toyota dealer, he could no longer resist the pull of his first love. He went back to school, this time to study design.

Diploma in hand, Kurokawa spent an interval testing the waters before joining Super Potato, a design agency with a reputation for creating innovative interiors. For two years he built models while taking every available opportunity to peek over the boss's shoulder. 'I learned a great deal from working with Sugimoto-san,' he says. During that time he met Masamichi Katayama, with whom he went on to establish a new agency, H-Design, in 1992. They worked as a team for eight intensively creative years, a period in which they made a name for themselves in and around Tokyo as sought-after specialists in interior and product design, before each decided to strike out on his own.

'My style has undergone a metamorphosis over the course of time,' says Kurokawa, looking back on his career. 'When I started out, interior design was still considered an art form. The designer made an interior so stunning that seeing it in a photograph made you want to see it in person. But not many of those designs were inviting enough to prompt a second visit. They were simply too beautiful – completely over the top.'

The kind of shop he describes is very complicated to make. A space that complex doesn't interest Kurokawa. 'I'd rather design a shop with a nice atmosphere, one that's not so stylistically arranged.' He tries to incorporate a sense of subtlety in his designs that prevents people from noticing immediately what it is that makes the shop special. Don't look for an impractical counter with a bizarre, in-your-face shape in a Kurokawa shop. And don't try to detect a uniform style in his designs. 'It's all about what the client wants,' he claims, 'and that's something

you have to approach in a creative manner.' Nor will you catch him following one trend after another. 'When I look at a space, I invariably see people in it. No matter what kind of clothes are for sale in that space, I want those people to be comfortable.

'White, high-tech interiors are still quite popular in Japan,' he continues, 'but I refuse to go with the flow. I often opt for dark colours and low-tech solutions.' A good example is No Concept But Good Sense, a shop in Harajuku that displays a diversity of furnishings, from gleaming transparent racks to a counter covered in old-fashioned rattan. What we see here could almost be defined as a 'no design' space. Of special interest are various details that are both functional and amusing. Theft-prevention mirrors double as light reflectors, for instance, and super magnets hold fashions in place. Kurokawa has a logical explanation: 'I wanted a space with no mannequins and walls free of railings and nails. The solution was magnets, which are flexible tools. At first I worried that they might not be strong enough, but it turns out that one of these magnets is capable of securing an object that weighs up to 20 kilograms.'

Kurokawa likes to combine old and new materials in his designs. 'It's interesting to make new materials look old and to recycle used materials,' he says. 'In Japan, where buildings are destroyed within a relatively short time span to make way for new structures, finding anything other than modern materials is not easy. Then, too, nearly every space I'm asked to design is new. Creating the desired ambience in Europe is not a big problem. Europe has so many old buildings whose interiors require nothing more than a simple layer of aluminium, plastic or white paint.' When working on a new-build project, Kurokawa often imbues the space with a sense of history by means of weathered, second-hand wood. He's used this method to 'age' the interiors of both Undercover and HOCQUY.

'WHITE, HIGH-TECH INTERIORS ARE QUITE POPULAR IN JAPAN, BUT I REFUSE TO GO WITH THE FLOW. I OFTEN OPT FOR DARK COLOURS AND LOW-TECH SOLUTIONS'

Walking the streets of Tokyo, studying people and their activities, breathing in the atmosphere of one vicinity or another – this is how the upbeat designer finds inspiration for his work.
'The ordinary things I see around the neighbourhood, the everyday events and chance encounters, are enough to feed my imagination. Inspiration used to mean being absolutely wild about the work of someone you admire, but it's not like that any more.'

The larger part of Kurokawa's practice, Out.Design, is located underground. The compact space has a functional layout. A narrow stairway with a view of an extremely tall, narrow window leads to a small room used for making models – a space that barely offers headroom to the average Western visitor. It hangs as a split-level volume halfway above the more deeply situated design studio. Daylight enters through a side window that looks out on a concrete wall.

International projects are on Kurokawa's wish list. Already in the making is a London bar. Although the design has been completed, British building regulations are holding up the works. 'Incredible how long we've been waiting for approval,' the designer sighs. 'A commercial project in Japan must be ready to open as quickly as possible. Follow the rules and that's it. In London, however, the process seems to go on forever.' In the meantime, he's hard at work designing shops for London fashion designer Chris Bailey – right here in the Land of the Rising Sun.

OUT.DESIGN
TSUTOMU KUROKAWA

黒川勉

NO CONCEPT BUT GOOD SENSE (FUKUOKA)

LOCATION
Wellbeing Building, 1F,
1-15-24 Ona, Chuo-ku,
Fukuoka
CLIENT
Lapine
FLOOR AREA
97 m²
START DESIGN
February 1999
OPENING
1 May 1999
INTERIOR ARCHITECT
Tsutomu Kurokawa
GENERAL CONSTRUCTOR
D.Brain Co.
LIGHTING DESIGN
Ushio Spax
FLOOR
vinyl flooring tile
WALL
plasterboard
CEILING
plasterboard
LIGHTING FIXTURES
Ushio Spax
SHOWCASE
stainless steel, glass
COUNTER
stainless steel, polycarbonate

PHOTOGRAPHY
Kozo Takayama

UNDERCOVER

LOCATION
Nowhere, 2F,
5-5-8 Minami-Aoyama, Minato-ku,
Tokyo
CLIENT
Undercover
FLOOR AREA
147 m²
START DESIGN
February 1999
OPENING
1 May 1999
INTERIOR ARCHITECT
Tsutomu Kurokawa
GENERAL CONSTRUCTOR
D.Brain Co.
LIGHTING DESIGN
Ushio Spax
ACTION PAINTER
Tsuyoshi Nakano
FLOOR
imported second-hand wood
WALL
plasterboard, stucco work
CEILING
plasterboard, stucco work
WINDOW
glass
LIGHTING FIXTURES
Ushio Spax
SOFA
Tsutomu Kurokawa
SEATING FABRIC
cotton (Undercover)
TABLE
fluorescent yellow acrylic
COUNTER
steel counter

PHOTOGRAPHY
Kozo Takayama

NO CONCEPT BUT GOOD SENSE (TOKYO)

LOCATION
6-30-3 Jingumae, Shibuya-ku,
Tokyo
CLIENT
Yamato International
FLOOR AREA
132 m²
START DESIGN
January 2000
OPENING
26 April 2000
INTERIOR ARCHITECT
Tsutomu Kurokawa
GENERAL CONSTRUCTOR
West
LIGHTING DESIGN
Ushio Spax
FLOOR
mortar, reinforced concrete,
painted moss green
WALL
steel, wood
CEILING
compressed teakwood
WINDOW
glass
LIGHTING FIXTURES
Ushio Spax
ACCESSORIES
spying mirrors,
magnets (up to 20-kg strength)
SHOWCASE
acrylic
COUNTER
rattan
SHOWCASE
steel

PHOTOGRAPHY
Kozo Takayama

HOCQUY

LOCATION
Garden Daikanyama, 1F,
16-15 Daikanyama-cho, Shibuya,
Tokyo
CLIENT
Gallery de Pop
FLOOR AREA
135 m²
START DESIGN
October 1999
OPENING
24 October 2000
INTERIOR ARCHITECT
Tsutomu Kurokawa
GENERAL CONSTRUCTOR
D.Brain Co.
LIGHTING DESIGN
Ushio Spax
FLOOR
stone, wood
WALL
plasterboard
CEILING
imported wood from London
WINDOW
glass, polycarbonate
LIGHTING FIXTURES
Ushio Spax
SEATING
Mapell chair
SEATING FABRIC
polycarbonate, wool, acrylic
DISPLAY TABLES
aluminium, wood
COUNTER
plywood
SHOWCASE
wood, steel, glass

PHOTOGRAPHY
Kozo Takayama

UTH

LOCATION
4-31-5 Jingumae, Shibuya-ku, Tokyo
CLIENT
LMEX House
FLOOR AREA
170 m²
START DESIGN
16 August
OPENING
16 December 2000
INTERIOR ARCHITECT
Tsutomu Kurokawa, Kanan Ogawa
GENERAL CONSTRUCTOR
Ask Planning Center
LIGHTING DESIGN
Ushio Spax
FLOOR
second hand wood (first floor);
stone (second floor)
WALL
stone
CEILING
concrete
WINDOW
glass
LIGHTING FIXTURES
Ushio Spax
LAMPS
Flow series (Tsutomu Kurokawa)
Sofa hanger SO-OIS: leather, stainless steel
COUNTER
aluminium
CHAIRS
stainless steel, wood

PHOTOGRAPHY
Kozo Takayama

OUT.DESIGN
102 MINAMI AOYAMA 3 HOUSE 3-3-1 MINAMI AOYAMA, MINATO-KU, TOKYO, 107-0062 JAPAN
T +81 (0)3-3746-0808 F +81 (0)3-3746-0505
E INFO@OUTDESIGN.COM WWW.OUTDESIGN.COM

NO CONCEPT BUT GOOD SENSE (FUKUOKA)

No Concept But Good Sense greets customers with a white fence and two doors bearing a large, simplistically illuminated logo. Tsutomu Kurokawa's clever design draws attention away from the unsightly façade of the building that houses the shop. Despite bright light streaming through the glass entrance doors, passers-by see nothing of what's going on inside. A sliding door at a severe slant completely conceals the view of the interior.

Inside, the womenswear line of this long-winded brand swims in a sea of immaculate whiteness. Gauzy, light-filtering curtains line the walls.

Except for the clothes rack at the centre of the space, all other furnishings seem to float in midair. Racks are mounted on the ceiling. The counter stands on a transparent base with illuminated legs. The only mirror in the shop sports casters and a nonchalant stainless-steel frame. Although the curtains do give the space a rather hospital-like environment, the shop has the kind of pleasant, delicate atmosphere aimed at restoring wellbeing.

UNDERCOVER

When asked to design the flagship store of casual streetwear brand Undercover, Tsutomu Kurokawa created a shop that could easily double as a gallery. Clothes racks function as a railing for the stairway into the shop.

Take the fashions away and little remains to remind us of a retail business. Walls display works of art. Furniture – such as a fluorescent green table and a sofa covered in fabric from Undercover's Vintage Collection – are positioned within the space like art installations. A steel staircase to the mezzanine adds a touch of industrial chic to the interior. What looks like a plain, glass-fronted concrete box on the outside could be, seen from the inside, the result of restoration done on a number of antique rooms.

Decorative beams on the 5-metre-high ceiling were imported from London, and the floor is made of used planks. Collaborating with Masamichi Katayama on this project, Kurokawa combined old and new in a recognisable way.

Drips of paint on the floor and 'F**k the Generation' in big letters were added later by fashion designer Jun Takahashi and a fellow artist. Thanks to windows on three sides and a skylight above the entrance stairs, the space is bathed in natural light during the day. Complementary fluorescent lighting prevents the space from being too warm and cosy. The client, an admirer of old London department stores, can move about this antiquated open space with satisfaction.

NO CONCEPT BUT GOOD SENSE (TOKYO)

Located on Meiji-dori, a busy thoroughfare in Tokyo, the shop is fronted by a narrow, often overcrowded strip of pavement. To distance the establishment from the chaotic street life, Kurokawa sacrificed some of the little retail space available. Placed at a slight slant, the glazed shop front is framed by sturdy steel pillars. The distinct demarcation between shop and jammed pavement cancels the need for a conventional shop window. Passers-by who glance up and spot the anti-theft mirrors above may well question the need for such equipment. Although they don't offer a clear view of the interior, the mirrors do pique our curiosity, however. Inside, the T-shaped rack at ground level is equipped with blinding spotlights aimed at the ceiling, where mirrors reflect the light from this central display unit. Kurokawa wanted a space without mannequins, which he felt would be counterproductive to the rough image of the shop. Walls clad in white steel hold magnetic hooks for displaying fashions. Upstairs, where both ceiling and walls are made of steel, merchandise is presented in the same innovative way. Kurokawa used these resources to create a sober, somewhat dark, low-tech ambience.

Wrapping up his design is the staircase, a steel colossus that hovers about 30 centimetres above the floor before suddenly swerving to meet a wooden step. We can almost hear him whisper, 'Did I calculate correctly?'

These strange stairs and the enormous variety of materials – from acrylic display units to rattan counter – imply a deliberate homage to bad taste. Or was this salmagundi born of necessity?

HOCQUY

The manufacturer is Japanese, the label is French and the client wanted a shop with Parisian allure. An environment that titillates all five senses. The image that designer Tsutomu Kurokawa had in mind was that of a French café, entirely open to the public. The large window he created tilts up to leave the façade completely free. A manual hoist determines the position of this cantilever window, and a tiled floor underscores the impression of a sidewalk café. Black pillars that support the air-conditioning column mark the transition from tiled to wooden floor. Together with the diagonally positioned aluminium wall behind the counter and the subdued lighting scheme, these dark elements prevent the space from having an obvious centre of attraction. Light from a ceiling-mounted clothes rack shines directly on the garments it holds. Counter and display cases balance on tenuous, steel-reinforced wooden legs. Visitors to the new outlet in Daikanyama's modern shopping complex should look at the ceiling, which is made of used wood, to discover a bit of history.

UTH

In designing the first shop in Japan to feature fashions by London designer Chris Bailey, Kurokawa envisioned a European look without a clear-cut style. The shop is in a narrow lane close to LaForet, the fashion centre of Tokyo's Harajuku district. Even though the façade projects from the building, it is modestly recessed in relation to the streetwall. Entering the shop, customers are immediately aware of Kurokawa's typical marriage of old and new materials. Used wood and brick contrast with gleaming leather. The integration of seating elements into clothes racks and display cases seems to be the theme of the design. A clothes rack attached to the back of a leather leather sofa is one example, as are wooden chairs installed on opposite sides of a showcase. Two shelving units are combined with a small sofa clad in black leather.

Although the result is a light-hearted and efficient use of space, the question remains: Does anyone actually sit on these seats? Leaning casually against a brick wall, a thick slab covered in rough canvas supports a clothes rack. It looks as though Kurokawa played a dangerous game with gravity and won: the object is perfectly balanced. The counter is accentuated by an aluminium openwork partition that also divides retail space from stockroom. A faux-escalator leads to the womenswear department upstairs. The illustration on these pages gives the false impression of a brick wall that clashes with the stone floor. In reality, the image is far more harmonious. The juxtaposition of these surfaces fits right in with Kurokawa's overall use of widely diverse materials.

SEI
MASARU ITO

伊藤 勝

With a modest smile, Masaru Ito offhandedly remarks that if things had gone a bit differently, he wouldn't be a designer at all. He initially planned to follow in his father's footsteps and become a doctor. 'But I failed the entrance exam,' he admits. 'It was just too difficult. So I set my sights on the field of art. My first choice was fine art, not design. I also had an interest in fashion – à la Miyake, Kawakubo and the like – but I thought I wasn't good enough. Going in that direction seemed like an insurmountable task.' After being admitted to the Tokyo University of Arts, Ito ultimately decided to study architecture. 'As a designer,' he says with a grin, 'I thought it might be easier to find a girlfriend.'

After six months of building models for Shin Takamatsu Architects in Kyoto, Ito had the good fortune to find a job with Takeo Kawasaki, a firm that put him directly to work with designers who were creating a shop for Comme des Garçons in Kichijoji. For five years, Kawasaki was his mentor. The first project Ito undertook on his own was a small office, but the big challenge came soon after in the form of a shop for CABANE de ZUCCa. 'We're talking about the very first CABANE de ZUCCa outlet,' says Ito. 'This was their flagship store. An extremely exciting moment.' Recently he designed a new flagship store for this fashion brand.

Located a stone's throw from the entertainment district of Roppongi, his studio is on the first floor of an old apartment building. A long corridor, low and dark, leads to a compact space divided in two by a partition of Venetian blinds. Despite a floor of old, sanded boards and a bookcase literally in scaffolding, the studio appears fresh and new. Contributing to this image is a brightly lit space that features a glass conference table and an austere, stainless-steel display case.
Clad in a glittery black shirt and artistically shabby black jeans, Ito is a man who claims a preference for materials that exhibit the ravages of time. 'A slightly crumbling wall, a rusty metal surface – there's something special about such things. I also like the look of a shop marked by several years of use. A bit of wear and tear adds an extra dimension to the interior.'

Unfortunately, interiors don't last very long in Japan. 'Tastes change every decade or so,' he says. 'That's only natural. But Japanese retailers have their premises refurbished far too often.' In Ito's opinion, this inconstancy stems from a milieu in which fashion is much more fleeting than it is in the rest of the world. 'In Japan you find young girls buying major brands like Hermes, Chanel and Prada, while in Europe it's the mature customer – a woman less sensitive to trends – who wears these labels. Shop interiors reflect this phenomenon. Here they're a bigger part of the fashion trend than they are in other countries.'

Ito tries to inject a sense of timelessness into the interiors he designs. His shops for fashion designer Issey Miyake, for example, draw inspiration from the new millennium. They take us on a journey into the future. Other designs offer an initial impression of raw emptiness and then surprise us with simple but intriguing interventions. Several shops with an almost bric-a-brac atmosphere display a pastiche of colour and decoration that seems to parody the cutesy atmosphere the Japanese call *kawaii*.

We detect no clear-cut direction in Ito's work. He's quick to agree. 'I'm more of a freestyle guy,' he admits. 'Each project has a lot to do with the client, of course, but my designs are as changeable as the weather.' In most cases, he adds little colour to the shops. 'The clothes should take centre stage, not the interior.' When it comes to materials, he's not afraid to experiment – 'I've been known to turn flooring tiles around and use the backs' – but he's not on a deliberate quest to find new materials.

Ito can't hide his enthusiasm when talking about his work. 'Some of the commissions I get are anything but fascinating to begin with, but within each project lies a challenge.' The words of a born optimist. Fascinating or humdrum, he starts with the basics. 'When it's a boutique, I check out the size of the fitting rooms and the storage area. Only then can I concentrate on the desired ambience. Sketches and models are geared to both budget and schedule. Occasionally we omit the model, because it's such a time-consuming element.' The realisation phase includes the inevitable struggle to satisfy building regulations.

'I LIKE THE LOOK OF A SHOP MARKED BY SEVERAL YEARS OF USE – A BIT OF WEAR AND TEAR ADDS AN EXTRA DIMENSION TO THE INTERIOR'

'But that goes with the territory,' he says. 'If you're not willing to fight that battle, you'll never make anything new, and what's important is the final result. Once the opening reception is over, so are your worries.'

In Ito's case, authorities and building regulations do not necessarily add up to a practical approach. He doesn't hesitate for a moment to take a design to extremes when presenting a rough draft of his concept. It's only later that he comes back to earth, plants both feet on the ground, and stops to consider how to implement his ideas, both technically and financially.

He mentions Mies van der Rohe, Philippe Starck and Rei Kawakubo as role models: 'All powerful figures, but I don't actually borrow from their work.' The designer finds music – from Tchaikovsky and Bach to John Lennon and Bob Marley – an even greater source of inspiration. 'Listening to music automatically leads to new ideas.'

On the subject of future work, what springs to Ito's mind are projects very close to home. He'd love to design a climbing frame and other play-related equipment for his child and, if opportunity knocks, to build a home for his own family.

SEI
MASARU ITO

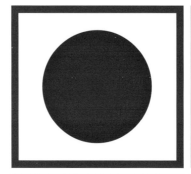

伊藤 勝

ISSEY MIYAKE MEN (SENDAI)

LOCATION
**Sendai Forus, B1F,
3-11-15, 1 Bancho, Aoba-ku, Sendai-shi,
Miyagi-ken**
CLIENT
Issey Miyake
FLOOR AREA
79 m²
START DESIGN
January 2000
OPENING
28 April 2000
INTERIOR ARCHITECT
Masaru Ito
GENERAL CONSTRUCTOR
Ishimaru
LIGHTING DESIGN
Masaru Ito
FLOOR
white linoleum
WALL
**plasterboard, transparent acrylic, stainless
steel frame**
CEILING
**plasterboard, transparent acrylic, stainless
steel frame**
LIGHTING FIXTURES
Zumtobel Staff
SEATING
Skeleton Mari-e
SHOWCASE CUBES
transparent acrylic
SHOWCASE
stainless steel, transparent acrylic

PHOTOGRAPHY
Nacása & Partners

ISSEY MIYAKE MEN (OSAKA)

LOCATION
**Abeno Kintetsu, 5F,
1-1-43, Abenosuji, Abeno-ku,
Osaka-shi**
CLIENT
Issey Miyake
FLOOR AREA
63 m²
START DESIGN
May 2000
OPENING
1 September 2000
INTERIOR ARCHITECT
Masaru Ito
GENERAL CONSTRUCTOR
Ishimaru
LIGHTING DESIGN
Masaru Ito
FLOOR
aluminium, glass light box, linoleum sheet
WALL
aluminium, plasterboard, glass light box
CEILING
plasterboard
LIGHTING FIXTURES
Zumtobel Staff
SHOWCASE
aluminium, acrylic

PHOTOGRAPHY
Nacása & Partners

ISSEY MIYAKE MEN (MATSUYA GINZA)

LOCATION
**Ginza Matsuya, 4F,
3-6-1 Ginza, Chuo-ku,
Tokyo**
CLIENT
Issey Miyake
INTERIOR ARCHITECT
Masaru Ito
GENERAL CONSTRUCTOR
Ishimaru, Mihoya Glass
LIGHTING DESIGN
Masaru Ito
FLOOR AREA
63 m²
START DESIGN
June 2000
OPENING
30 September 2000
FLOOR
concrete
WALL
plasterboard, acrylic emergent paint
CEILING
plasterboard, acrylic emergent paint
LIGHTING FIXTURES
Koizumi
SHOWCASE
stainless steel, glass

PHOTOGRAPHY
Nacása & Partners

FRIDGE STORE

LOCATION
**La Fuente, 1F,
11-1 Sarugaku-cho, Shibuya-ku,
Tokyo**
CLIENT
A-Net
FLOOR AREA
46 m²
START DESIGN
October 2000
OPENING
9 December 2000
ARCHITECT
Kashima Kensetsu
INTERIOR ARCHITECT
Masaru Ito
GENERAL CONSTRUCTOR
Ishimaru
LIGHTING DESIGN
Masaru Ito
FLOOR
concrete
WALL
plasterboard
CEILING
concrete
WINDOW
glass
LIGHTING FIXTURES
Max Ray
FITTING ROOM SCREEN
steel gas pipe, cotton
SHOWCASE
acrylic, steel, glass, artificial grass sheets

PHOTOGRAPHY
Nacása & Partners

SEI

MIKAWADAI HEIGHTS 101, 4-3-6 ROPPONGI, MINATO-KU, TOKYO, 106-0032 JAPAN

T +81 (0)3-5785-3681 F +81 (0)3-5785-3682

E SEI@A5599.COM

SEI SEI SEI SEI SEI SEI SEI SEI SEI SEI SEI SEI SEI SEI SEI SEI SEI SEI SEI SEI SEI SEI SEI SEI SEI SEI SEI SEI SEI SEI SEI SEI SEI SEI SEI SEI SEI SEI SEI SEI SEI SEI SEI SEI SEI SEI SEI SEI SEI SEI SEI SEI SEI SEI SEI SEI SEI SEI SEI SEI SEI SEI SEI

ISSEY MIYAKE MEN (SENDAI)

Partially hidden below ground level and housed in the Sendai Forus department store is a shop that the unsuspecting passer-by will not soon forget. A small transparent volume emerges from a corner of the shopping complex – a frame with rounded profiles that transforms Issey Miyake Men into an elegant peep shop. By making its structure in stainless steel, however, Masaru Ito reinforced the potency of Miyake's menswear line. The rest of the space is largely transparent. Shelving, tables and display cases made of a clear acrylic material allow all attention to focus on the predominantly dark colours of the current collection. A visitor to the compact space feels enveloped in a snug cocoon. The main disadvantage of Ito's interior design is that acrylic resin attracts dust. Employees have a full-time job just keeping this extraordinary globular shop spick-and-span.

ISSEY MIYAKE MEN (OSAKA)

In early 2000, a 30-year-old Stanley Kubrick film became the impetus for an up-to-date design project in which Ito tried to express what the director had in mind when making *A Space Odyssey: 2001*. The pivotal element is Spacy, a lighting system built into floor and ceiling. Ito's retail concept included a floor made entirely of glass, but his client, Issey Miyake, was afraid that a see-through foundation might put people off. Located in the menswear section of a large department store, Miyake's shop-in-a-shop is far more conspicuous than its neighbours. A slight elevation at the entrance leads to six brightly lit floorboards of frosted glass. The same type of glass panel has been installed beneath a display rail for clothes on hangers. The rest of the floor, as well as the furnishings, has a mat-silver finish that gives the space a rarefied, industrial ambience: a cross between a laboratory and a spaceship. This project can be seen as an elaboration on the Miyake shop in Sendai. Here, however, Ito reduced the size of the spherical forms he used. Boldly positioned in a diagonal direction are three tall display units and one lower unit. 'Dot' lights behind the counter boast a high-tech look but are, in fact, ordinary low-tech reflector lamps: an amusing point of relief in an otherwise subdued environment.

ISSEY MIYAKE MEN

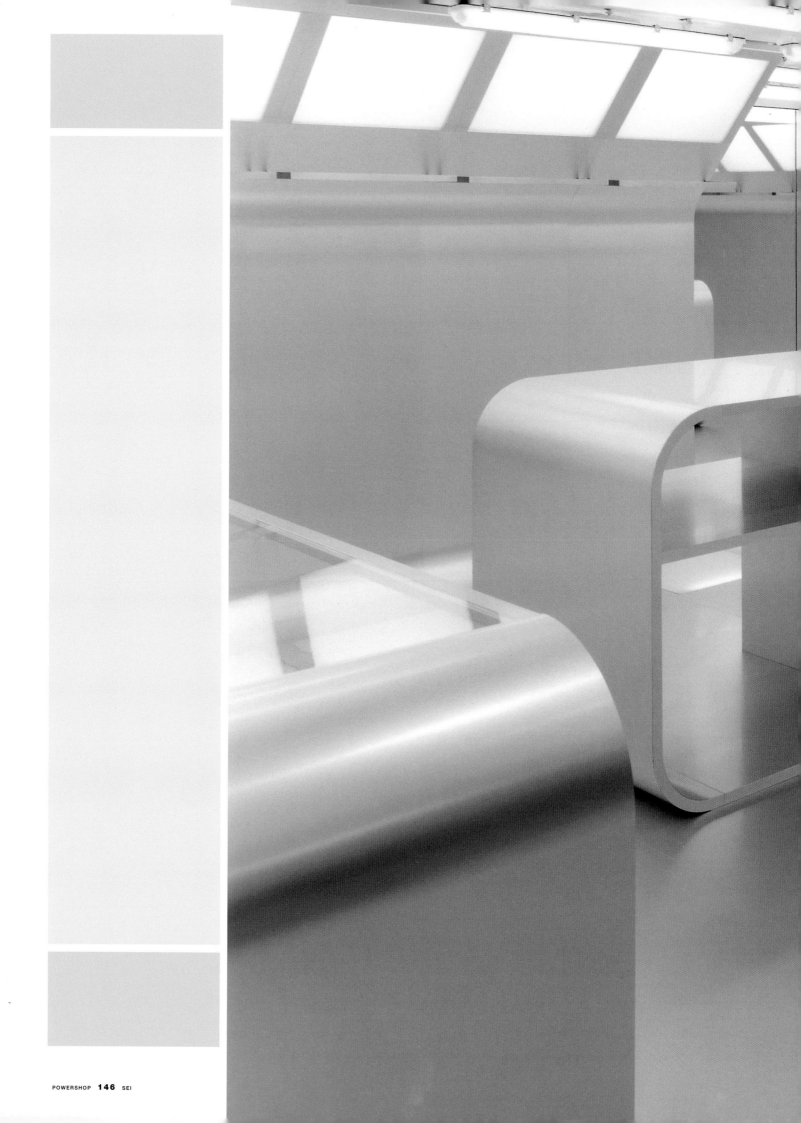

ISSEY MIYAKE MEN (MATSUYA GINZA)

In designing the third in a series of shops for Issey Miyake, Masaru Ito again turned to his passion for glass. His initial idea – a space composed of nothing but glass, featuring items of clothing individually and literally encased in glass – proved to be financially infeasible. He had also planned to cut each glass panel into a unique concave shape. The finished project, however, has little to do with his original concept. Hanging garments are interrupted by protruding, rounded glass panels. Between and behind the clothing Ito mounted sets of four glass fins on the wall.

The rhythm established by these fins is reinforced by three glass display tables whose tops rest on latticework bases. These objects subtly exhibit the natural green gradation of the glass, which lends a touch of warmth to this rather austere space. Three additional display units are composed of glass and stainless steel. A simple concrete floor complements the muted effect of the greenish glass and, in differing from the wooden floor of the reputable department store that accommodates this shop, distinguishes the interior from its surroundings.

FRIDGE STORE

A large display window provides a nice view of the interior, but where's the entrance to Fridge Shop? I pass two other shops before spotting an open door next to a lift. A long narrow corridor is the prelude to a retail space the size of a postage stamp. Apart from the display window, I could be in the well-hidden broom closet of this contemporary building. A bright green strip of artificial grass running along a white wall is the backdrop for Hershey-chocolate candles and little dolls labelled 'final home'. The window at the far end of the space features a wide sill and three steps. Masaru Ito basically left the premises as he found them, adding a bare minimum of elements to enliven the atmosphere. Envisioning the space as a continuous aisle, he mounted rails on the ceiling, used a portable screen to cordon off a fitting area and thus created room for customers to walk around and examine the merchandise. Despite its diminutive proportions, the shop proves to be a surprisingly good showcase for designer Koisuke Tsumura's experimental fashions.

WONDERWALL
MASAMICHI KATAYAMA

片山 正通

A leather Louis Vuitton football in a net dangles nonchalantly from the hat stand. Innumerable CDs and books line long shelves in a space that also accommodates a comfortable sitting area, a fireplace, an Eames Lounge Chair and a gigantic album of photographs by Helmut Newton. Display cases sparkle with accessories that vary from expensive watches to little plastic dolls. Prominently positioned in the room are huge photos of two women urinating man-style against a wall. Welcome to the office of self-professed shopping fanatic Masamichi Katayama.

'I'm absolutely crazy about shopping,' he says. 'The last time I was in Milan, I spent more time in the city than at the famous furniture fair. I'm not really interested in looking at what other furniture designers have done. I'd rather go into town and browse around. It's hard for me to walk down the street without stopping to buy a CD or a book.' If I'm to judge by his vast collection of objects, he must walk down quite a few shopping streets. 'Electronics, CDs, books – these are my toys. Buying something can really make my day. That's why I enjoy retail design so much. I'm totally familiar with the ins and outs of shopping.'

Katayama, who calls his company Wonderwall, sees shopping as entertainment. 'It's amusement, like Disneyland. It's got to be exciting. The term that fits the situation is "time service". As a designer, I find it a challenge to lure people into a shop and keep them there for 10 to 20 minutes. I balance on the edge between a space that has a good atmosphere and one that doesn't. A design that goes to extremes is all right in a city like Tokyo,' the designer assures me. 'A newly designed boutique in Milan, for example, will be around ten years or so before it's renovated. In Japan it's five years at most and, on average, about three. The short time span allows for more risk. The design represents a single moment in time.'

He tries to create spaces that get noticed, that give customers the feeling that they're involved in something special. 'I want them to leave the shop just dying to tell their friends about it.' He definitely hit the mark with A Bathing Ape, a chain that has achieved cult status among the teenage crowd in recent years.

Stripped of both signage and shop windows, these outlets began the journey to fame and fortune by being nearly impossible for anyone to locate – with the exception, of course, of those in the know. Once inside, however, the customer surprisingly finds a clearly illuminated space backed by a cheerful, cool design. Katayama saw each of the 11 BAPE shops (BAPE being the abbreviated version of this streetwear label) as a king-size challenge. 'Nothing we dreamed up and eventually realised was according to the book,' he admits. Today's visit to a BAPE shop is no longer an underground activity, but constant change is something that continues to be part of the BAPE formula.

'The time you spend in a shop should be pleasant,' says the designer. 'The good feeling I'm talking about differs for every target group. Discovering and developing the desired ambience is what retail design is all about.' In his projects for fashion designer Marc Jacobs, Katayama took a relatively subdued approach. And when designing restaurants, he omits the shock effect altogether. 'These are places in which you spend several hours. The environment should be relaxing and not overly stimulating.'

Katayama had no interest in design as a youngster. He ended up in the field more or less by accident. Hoping that he would later take over the family furniture shop, his father sent him to design school. But to the surprise of both, Katayama ended up taking courses in interior design. 'After joining a construction firm, my first job was to help design the interior of a dental practice,' he recalls. 'Incredibly boring.' He decided to try his luck in Tokyo, but finding his niche wasn't easy. He answered to one boss after another before testing the waters of freelance design. Japan's bubble economy burst around that time, leaving him and others like him madly swimming against the tide.

The turn-around came when he and Tsutomu Kurokawa teamed up to establish H-Design. Gradually a steady flow of projects came their way, and after a few years of creative collaboration, they decided to see what each could achieve on his own. Currently Katayama is one of Japan's more productive

'AS A DESIGNER, I FIND IT A CHALLENGE TO LURE PEOPLE INTO A SHOP AND KEEP THEM THERE FOR 10 TO 20 MINUTES'

retail designers. He manages to design the interiors of an amazing 70 or so shops each year. Every design begins with a concept, and the rest of the work is based on a logical development of this idea. Take the And A shops, for example, which have a cube as their point of departure. Even the cubic hooks on the clothes hangers correspond to Katayama's basic concept. It's as if he's trying to force us to recognise the underlying idea. Other concepts include an American deli and a sweet shop – the latter is the theme of a retail shoe store. And in yet another case Katayama took his cue from the client, IS Sunao Kuwahara, a fashion brand that often features apparel turned inside out. Here he turned his materials around and used the backs to underline the concept of the clothing in the shop.

He limits the number of materials in his projects, and the resulting simplicity can be overwhelming. Everyone sees immediately what he had in mind; Katayama has no use for complicated technological tricks. 'I make designs that everyone can understand,' he says. 'Behind the scenes things may get a little complex, but that's something I try to conceal.' Selecting materials is not an essential part of his work. 'The materials I choose depend on the concept I'm working with. I'm very much into lighting, however. Light can be compared to scent or sound. It's not something you experience directly, but it's there, and the designer puts it there. Lighting is also a cost-control material. Even when inexpensive, it can be highly effective. In our design for IS Sunao Kuwahara, for example, we used 100 ordinary light bulbs at 2.6 euros each. For only 264 euros we created a fantastic visual effect without going over our very tight budget.'

Katayama has no desire to design domestic interiors. 'If a client who's just built a new house asks for something deep red, for instance, you can't say that it's a grotesque colour or that it just doesn't work in that space. The client has to live there and look at it day after day. When you take on a job like that, you're more of a technician involved in the building process than a creative contributor.' Katayama finds hotels a more interesting idea. 'A hotel is a meeting point, not a place intended for daily life. It has a field of tension you can work with.'

Katayama is currently setting out a new course, which goes beyond the shores of Japan. 'I did a project in Hong Kong, and I wouldn't mind working in Europe,' he says. 'But my home base is and remains Japan. This country is filled with shoppers who think nothing of paying 880 euros for a little jacket they'll wear for only one season, while eating instant noodles at home that cost them a mere 0.9 euros. Where else are people willing to spend so much money to flaunt a hip image?'

WONDERWALL
MASAMICHI KATAYAMA

片山 正通

I.S. SUNAO KUWAHARA

LOCATION
**La Fuente, 1F,
11-1 Sarugaku-cho, Shibuya-ku,
Tokyo**
CLIENT
A-Net
FLOOR AREA
136 m²
START DESIGN
July 2000
OPENING
9 December 2000
ARCHITECT
Kashima Kensetsu
INTERIOR ARCHITECT
Masamichi Katayama
GENERAL CONSTRUCTOR
Ishimaru
LIGHTING DESIGN
Masamichi Katayama
FLOOR
unpolished Japanese cedar wood
WALL
black paint
CEILING
skeleton
WINDOW
glass
LIGHTING FIXTURES
Ushio Spax
COUNTER
wood, black paint
SHELVING
cedar wood, glass

PHOTOGRAPHY
Kozo Takayama

AND A

LOCATION
**1-19-29, Minami-Horie, Nishi-ku,
Osaka**
CLIENT
And A
FLOOR AREA
467 m²
START DESIGN
December 2000
OPENING
1 March 2001
INTERIOR ARCHITECT
Masamichi Katayama
GENERAL CONSTRUCTOR
Daimaru Mokko
LIGHTING DESIGN
**Masamichi Katayama, Masaki Yasuhara
(Ushio Spax)**
FLOOR
**black-painted concrete, glass (first floor);
aluminium (second floor)**
WALL
black-painted plasterboard
CEILING
**white-painted plasterboard, acrylic light
box cubes (first floor); black painted
plasterboard, acrylic light box cubes
(second floor)**
WINDOW
glass
LIGHTING FIXTURES
Ushio Spax
CUBE SOFA
black canvas
COUNTER
aluminium
SHOWCASES
aluminium, glass
SHELVING
aluminium, white paint

PHOTOGRAPHY
Kozo Takayama

A BATHING APE BUSY WORK SHOP

LOCATION
**4-28-22 Jingumae, Shibuya-ku,
Tokyo**
CLIENT
Nowhere
FLOOR AREA
138 m²
START DESIGN
May 2001
OPENING
July 15, 2001
INTERIOR ARCHITECT
Masamichi Katayama
GENERAL CONSTRUCTOR
D.Brain Co.
LIGHTING DESIGN
Masamichi Katayama
FLOOR
aluminium, glass (2 x 8mm)
WALL
**painted plasterboard,
polished stainless steel**
CEILING
**painted plasterboard, stainless steel,
indirect lighting**
LIGHTING FIXTURES
Ushio Spax
ACCESSORIES
Sony monitor
COUNTER
stainless steel
TABLE
polished stainless steel
HANGER PIPE
stainless steel

PHOTOGRAPHY
Kozo Takayama

SONY TOWER (3F AND 4F)

LOCATION
**Sony Tower, 3F/4F,
1-1-10 Shinsaibashi-suji, Chuo-ku,
Osaka-shi, Osaka**
CLIENT
Sony Corporation
FLOOR AREA
308 m²
START DESIGN
June 2001
OPENING
2 August 2001
ARCHITECT
Kisho Kurokawa
INTERIOR ARCHITECT
Masamichi Katayama
GENERAL CONSTRUCTOR
Hakusuisha
LIGHTING DESIGN
**Masamichi Katayama, Masaki Yasuhara
(Ushio Spax)**
FLOOR
white stone, aluminium
WALL
painted plasterboard, screen glass
CEILING
**painted plasterboard, plastered,
39 Sony flat panel monitors**
WINDOW
glass
LIGHTING FIXTURES
Ushio Spax
MONITOR FRAMES
stainless steel
SEATING
**LC2 (Le Corbusier), Juli, Hudson,
aluminium desk chair**
COUNTER
stainless steel
SHOWCASE
stainless steel, acrylic
BENCH
orange vinyl leather
TABLE
aluminium
DISPLAY TABLE
acrylic, mirrored stainless steel

PHOTOGRAPHY
Kozo Takayama

FOOTSOLDIER

LOCATION
Kumoshita Building, 1F, 3-7 Sakuraku-cho, Shibuya-ku, Tokyo
CLIENT
FootSoldier
FLOOR AREA
210 m²
START DESIGN
May 2001
OPENING
1 October 2001
INTERIOR ARCHITECT
Masamichi Katayama
GENERAL CONSTRUCTOR
D.Brain Co.
LIGHTING DESIGN
Masamichi Katayama, Masaki Yasuhara (Ushio Spax)
FLOOR
wool carpet (Masamichi Katayama)
WALL
black-painted plasterboard
CEILING
black-painted plasterboard
WINDOW
glass
LIGHTING FIXTURES
Ushio Spax
COUNTER
stainless steel, glass, mirror
SHOWCASE
stainless steel, glass
BENCH
vinyl leather, mirrored stainless steel
SHOE CONVEYER BELT
stainless steel, glass

PHOTOGRAPHY
Kozo Takayama

WONDERWALL
1-21-18 EBISU-MINAMI, SHIBUYA-KU, TOKYO, 150-0022 JAPAN
T +81 (0)3-5725-8989 F +81 (0)3-5725-8988
E KATAYAMA@WONDER-WALL.COM WWW.WONDER-WALL.COM

I.S. SUNAO KUWAHARA

Take an army of light bulbs – let's say 100 or so – with standard metal frames and mount them on the exposed structure of a ceiling: Masamichi Kurokawa wondered if the impact would match that of Alfred Hitchcock's terrifying *Birds*. Although I don't find it particularly frightening, it is quite impressive.
A black wall at the rear of the shop and a floor and wardrobes of unfinished wood are a good match for the rather coarse, makeshift look of the fashions sold here. Katayama designed the interiors of another twenty I.S. outlets in the past four years, all of which feature the same sort of basic, unrefined materials. Light bulbs, unfinished floors, ordinary hangers and simple wooden shelving add up to what might be called an 'eco' environment. For this project, the designer has exaggerated the bare lighting design to such a degree that it becomes an agreeable accessory.
A glass storefront higher than the ceiling inside makes the raw interior skeleton part of the picture seen by passers-by. A sliding door is the only opaque section of the façade. Take a simple light bulb, multiply it by 100, get a surprising effect, spend next to nothing – surely this is the way to a client's heart!

AND A

A pitch-black façade on a peaceful street in Osaka's hip Minami-Horie district glowers like an impenetrable fortress. Visitors follow a narrow rectangular tunnel of glass to gain access to the monochrome world of And A. This shop is a recalcitrant response to the current spate of curvilinear interiors and an emphatic homage to the cube. Masamichi Katayama collaborated with Frenchman Ramdane Touhami to develop a theme that harks back to the angular '80s. Black surfaces above, below and on all sides are in stark contrast to ceiling-mounted cube lamps and an illuminated mat-glass floor at the rear of the shop. A centrally positioned faux garden with an emerald-green surface of artificial grass brusquely interrupts the flow of black and white. Several groups of casually arranged black cubes reflect their white counterparts on the ceiling. Ascend to the upper level to find a negative of the black-and-white world below. What's white downstairs is black upstairs. Here a balustrade and a void offer intriguing views of the cubic shop. Furnishings such as the slender, one-footed showcases are also part of the squared-off theme. Even the coat-hanger hooks sport a 90-degree angle. One display unit upstairs gives the space a splash of colour. Like the imitation garden below, it's the only element that refuses to play the game of black and white. Lighting on each shelf of this unit matches the colour of the product displayed. The result is a cosy spot that warms an otherwise uncompromising space

A BATHING APE BUSY WORK SHOP

An inconspicuous flight of stairs leading to an underground shop attracted a lot of attention in recent years, thanks to the vast numbers of teenagers waiting to get in. Like kids lining up for popular rides at Disneyland, even after entering the shop these customers remained in the queue, which reached all the way to the back of the space. Masamichi Katayama actually integrated the 'queue' concept into his design, which featured a long, dark corridor that opened into an astonishing interior, creating a shock effect that drew hordes of enthusiastic visitors to A Bathing Ape. Three years after the opening, the owner called on Katayama to conjure up a new surprise. The designer rotated the interior 180 degrees, added a sliding door of opaque white glass and a vestibule, and provided the client with a more accessible shop. The counter, which looks as if it was born in an American deli, and a poster rack for T-shirts – neither of which is standard equipment in the world of boutiques – are now icons of the brand. A mirrored wall at the rear visually increases the dimensions of these compact premises. The new point of curiosity is also at the back of the rectangular space, where customers can stand on a glass surface and look down into a maze of white pipes beneath their feet. Inspired by the film *Blade Runner*, Katayama blatantly exposed the guts of the building. The initial impression is one of a floor that has been broken open. Hesitatingly, customers tiptoe onto the 'ice', hoping they won't fall through. Less adventurous souls first grasp the aluminium fencing around the glass floor. If Katayama was out to create excitement and sensation, this brainchild is the proof of his success.

SONY TOWER (3F AND 4F)

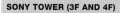

For the renovation of its Osaka showroom, Sony wanted a soft yet ultramodern look. Two months before the reopening, the electronics emperor commissioned Masamichi Katayama to design the interior of the narrow, two-storey space, which he transformed into brightly illuminated experimental gardens. One floor is devoted to broadband telecommunication.
The designer based his concept on a world without gravity. After all, the ever-accelerating transmission of data made possible by broadband technology is lighter than air and wholly intangible. He aimed for a sense of weightlessness, which he realised by creating ceiling-mounted tables that don't touch the ground and a seating design that relies on a single slender leg.

Mat-glass partitions separate computers and allow visitors to try out all sorts of e-commerce services in relative privacy. Mat-glass walls clad in a special film display projected images without dominating the space. Indirect lighting from both ceiling and display units illuminates the showroom. A small, transparent studio for special events claims the centre of the space.
In the seating area, which offers a view of the busy street outside, laptops with internet connections are ready for use. On another level, visitors can experiment with all sorts of new electronic equipment presented on a row of reflective metal cubes. The display surfaces are finished in glass and illuminated from within.

Passers-by have a good view of what is probably the most expensive modular ceiling in the world. Flat plasma panels are mounted on the ceiling upstairs. The 37 monitors cost a total of 55.5 million yen (nearly 500,000 euros). From outside the building, mini-films flashing across these screens look extremely impressive. Visitors inside, however, hardly notice the monitors, which are embedded quite unobtrusively into the ceiling. Only the heat they emit draws attention to the space above.

The American coffee concern Starbucks has a shop one level beneath the showroom. Visitors may sip their cappuccino upstairs in the sterile, white space belonging to Sony, while relaxing in white-leather Le Corbusier chairs and viewing trailers for Hollywood's latest blockbusters. Spilling hot coffee on a brand-new laptop in this posh environment is definitely a no-no, however. Perhaps it's better to drink your brew downstairs before going up to admire the functional quality of Katayama's sleek, uncomplicated interior.

sony style

sony style

Sony Travel

Broadband Community Gate

FOOTSOLDIER

A sneaker shop that doesn't look like a sneaker shop – that was the essence of the brief. Katayama, who had designed the interior of A Bathing Ape for the same client, immediately proposed the idea of a brightly hued patisserie. He designed a candy-coloured carpet and painted the rest of the space black to accentuate the vibrant floor. The rear wall features five big plasma monitors for showing clever computer animations. Reflective bases on the spacious seating elements mirror the design of the ten-tinted floor covering, thus creating a continuously carpeted effect. As you walk past leather sofas, sinking deeper into the richly piled carpet with each step, it's hard to believe that Katayama's white alcoves are filled with canvas sneakers or even the latest Nike styles. Nor do you expect to be confronted with a quiet parade of footwear gliding by on a stainless-steel conveyor belt. Moving in a lazy circle, the belt – enclosed in a king-size oval showcase – displays one pair of shoes after another, most of which stand on low pedestals that hold them in place. A sheet of stainless steel bearing the shop logo embraces the huge object, which reminds me of *kaiten sushi* (inexpensive Japanese restaurants that display their dishes on tiny conveyor belts). Admittedly, Footsoldier's example has a more sophisticated flair.
Here the shoes are presented as objects too precious to touch, much less to wear. Everything about the place conveys the same message: We're not here to sell you ordinary shoes.

HIDEO YASUI ATELIER
HIDEO YASUI

安井 秀夫

Even as a child, Hideo Yasui was a creative builder. 'My father had a construction company, and I became familiar with building and architecture at a very early age.' Years later, armed with a diploma in architecture, a still youthful Yasui joined the Azuma Construction Company, where he spent four years as a trainee before leaving to gain more experience in interior design at Kitaoka. The career move turned out to be a stroke of good luck, as it led to his involvement in the first of Yohji Yamamoto's shops in Japan and New York. 'The shops we designed at that time were rather robust and not very inviting,' he recalls. 'Even the personnel were not particularly accommodating. Our designs were just the opposite of the slick interiors so popular in those days.' Coincidentally, Yasui's current office – on the sixth floor of a standard block of flats – is a mere 200 metres from the main Yohji Yamamoto outlet in Tokyo's Minami Aoyama district. In the office four assistants sit in complete silence, fingers on their keyboards, surrounded by stacks of papers, books and magazines.

'When I started my own business in 1988, my first project was a house for good friends. I've continued to design private homes ever since, as well as the occasional commercial space.' His work ranges from shops and beauty salons to restaurants and medical clinics, but each space is characterised by Yasui's deep interest in light, both natural and artificial. Dark, unilluminated corners are virtually nonexistent. Transparency and lucid indirect lighting are his trademarks. One of his sources of inspiration is Louis Kahn, architect and lighting expert par excellence, whose work Yasui discovered while still an architecture student.

Pictures of buildings and architectonic theories set down in books are not enough for Yasui, however. He'd rather travel and see the real thing. The Middle East, with its venerable architecture and ancient cities, is a favourite destination. 'Particularly fascinating are the souks [marketplaces in Muslim countries],' he says. 'The extraordinary incidence of light…that depth…magnificent.' His words brim with enthusiasm. 'It's hot there. Vendors protect themselves from the sun, but they still have to allow light to enter the space. So exciting.' He mentions

Greece as well, a country in which sunlight falls on houses white as sheets. And the first light that wakes you on Sunday morning. He looks for different qualities of light and tries to reproduce them in his designs. 'Light may have no focus. It may blind you. But it's light that paints the space. That's the kind of light I want to re-create in my projects.'

Wherever possible, Yasui tries to incorporate daylight into his work. And if natural light is not an option, he uses indirect lighting. 'Satin Doll, for example, is illuminated completely with artificial light,' he says. 'I spotlighted the space from above and below. By keeping the walls free, I made the narrow space look somewhat broader and calmer.' The impassioned 'man of light' also draws inspiration from people and objects outside his profession. 'I'm absolutely mesmerised, for instance, by the Japanese footballer Nakata, who's currently playing in Italy. You can sense his focused determination to succeed internationally as he heads for the goal and scores. A thrilling experience.'

Yasui's own goals are at the interface of public and commercial spaces, an area that includes such disparate projects as museum cafés and urban-planning schemes. It's an area still in its infancy in Japan. 'Public projects in this country are so bogged down by restrictions that they're really not worth the bother,' the architect explains. 'At the MoMA in New York, on the other hand, they've realised that another approach is possible. MoMA's innovatively designed café, for example, which features work by Droog Design, is open to the general public and not just to museum visitors.' Another project that Yasui sees as a challenge is an urban plan for the area adjacent to a public-transport station. He's already made a number of drafts for local authorities, but none has been realised. Yasui has participated in the design of other public spaces as well. In consultation with neighbourhood residents, he created colourful toilet facilities in a playground park. 'Toilet areas are usually dark and dirty. My design is filled with fresh air and daylight. It has engendered such pride among residents that they keep the building clean on their own initiative.'

'THE FIRST LIGHT THAT WAKES YOU ON SUNDAY MORNING IS SOMETHING I TRY TO REPRODUCE. LIGHT MAY HAVE NO FOCUS. IT MAY BLIND YOU. BUT IT'S LIGHT THAT PAINTS THE SPACE'

In addition to his love of light, Yasui likes working with aluminium because of its flexibility. 'I like the cool image – rather hip and detached – that I can produce with aluminium,' he says. 'And it's both durable and cheap – two more plus points.' His earlier preference for plastic, especially acrylic, has made way for an interest in wood. And when he opts for glass, it's usually to lend a sense of invisibility to something like shelves or cabinets. 'But to give such objects a little bit of body,' he says, 'I often stretch a length of lace or a layer of film between two sheets of glass. Doing that makes the lace or the film the special component and not the glass.'

When working in retail design, Yasui sees it as his task to get people into the shop and to make them want to stay there. 'The atmosphere has to be somewhat unusual, or they'll walk right out again.' His use of voids and split levels to enlarge a space optically is an efficient strategy. It draws the visitor into the space. In his opinion, shop windows are not the answer. 'Window shopping as practised in the West is a rare occurrence in Japan. Everybody here goes into the shop. So it's important for the place to radiate a warm welcome and to hold the shopper's attention. Only then will the Japanese buy.'

He's not much of a shopper himself. 'I don't stroll from store to store without a purpose. The joy of making a purchase comes only when I buy a product I really want. And that's not a random event that occurs while I'm browsing around and accidentally find something nice to take home.'

A remarkable aspect of Yasui's work – an aspect that seems to clash with the prevailing trend in Japan – is that his buildings are in harmony with the immediate surroundings. A Yasui design doesn't stand out because it has a dramatic colour scheme or because it towers over its neighbours. Only the form of the building, subtle and unpretentious, catches the eye. Yasui himself prefers not to discuss style or a particular approach to design. Faced with a new project, he reviews his arsenal of materials and gives little thought to style. 'Let someone else put a label on it.'

HIDEO YASUI ATELIER
HIDEO YASUI

安井 秀夫

D'GRACE (FUKUOKA)

LOCATION
B2F, Tenjin Vivre,
1-11-1 Tenjin, Chuo-ku,
Fukuoka-shi
CLIENT
P/X
FLOOR AREA
125 m²
START DESIGN
May 1998
OPENING
August 1998
INTERIOR ARCHITECT
Hideo Yasui
GENERAL CONSTRUCTOR
OB
LIGHTING DESIGN
Hideo Yasui
FLOOR
vinyl tile
WALL
polycarbonate
CEILING
painted plasterboard
LIGHTING FIXTURES
Daiko
SHOWCASES
acrylic, polycarbonate

PHOTOGRAPHY
Nacása & Partners

SATIN DOLL

LOCATION
3-24-7 Shinjuku, Shinjuku-ku,
Tokyo
CLIENT
Fuji Fur Inc.
INTERIOR ARCHITECT
Hideo Yasui
GENERAL CONSTRUCTOR
Biruto
LIGHTING DESIGN
Hideo Yasui
FLOOR AREA
34 m²
START DESIGN
July 1998
OPENING
October 1998
FLOOR
aluminium
WALL
steel paint on plasterboard
LIGHTING FIXTURES
Daiko
COUNTER
aluminium counter
SHOWCASE
crystal glass

PHOTOGRAPHY
Nacása & Partners

LA CIENEGA

LOCATION
2-2-5 Oote, Matsumoto-shi,
Nagano
CLIENT
La Cienega Co., Ichiro Kamiyama
FLOOR AREA
164 m²
START DESIGN
January 1998
OPENING
March 1999
ARCHITECT
Hideo Yasui
INTERIOR ARCHITECT
Hideo Yasui
GENERAL CONSTRUCTOR
Okaken Kogyo
LIGHTING DESIGN
Hideo Yasui
FLOOR
aluminium, marble stone
WALL
concrete
CEILING
steel
WINDOW
glass
LIGHTING FIXTURES
Daiko
COUNTER
aluminium, glass
SHOWCASE
laced glass, polycarbonate

PHOTOGRAPHY
Nacása & Partners

FEMME ET MODE

LOCATION
1-3-52 Ohmachi, Yuzawa-shi,
Akita
CLIENT
Mogami Tazaemon
FLOOR AREA
483 m²
START DESIGN
August 1997
OPENING
September 1999
INTERIOR ARCHITECT
Hideo Yasui
GENERAL CONSTRUCTOR
Kumagai Kensetsu
LIGHTING DESIGN
Hideo Yasui
FLOOR
marble stone
WALL
painted plasterboard
CEILING
painted plasterboard, plated glass
WINDOW
glass
LIGHTING FIXTURES
Daiko
COUNTER
aluminium
SHOWCASE
glass

PHOTOGRAPHY
Nacása & Partners

D'GRACE (SENDAI FORUS)

LOCATION
**Sendai Forus, 3F,
3-11-15, 1 Bancho, Aoba-ku, Sendai-shi,
Miyagi-ken**
CLIENT
P/X
FLOOR AREA
73 m²
START DESIGN
January 2000
OPENING
4 March 2000
INTERIOR ARCHITECT
Hideo Yasui
GENERAL CONSTRUCTOR
Arenz Craft
LIGHTING DESIGN
Hideo Yasui
FLOOR
aluminium
WALL
painted plasterboard
CEILING
painted plasterboard
LIGHTING FIXTURES
Daiko
SHOWCASE
glass, silk screen sheets

PHOTOGRAPHY
Nacása & Partners

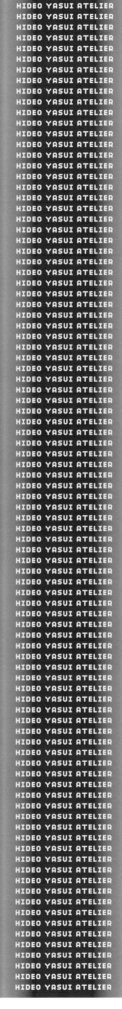

HIDEO YASUI ATELIER

6-1-32 604 MINAMI AOYAMA, MINATO-KU, TOKYO, 107-0062 JAPAN
T +81 (0)3-3498-5633 F +81 (0)3-5466-7621
E YASUIA@BLUE.OCN.NE.JP WWW.DESIGN-LIFE.COM/YASUIA

D'GRACE (FUKUOKA)

Deep underground – beneath a hip department store in Fukuoka geared to Japanese youth – lies a boutique with an absolutely dazzling interior designed by Hideo Yasui. What the client had in mind was a more grown-up image for fashion brand D'Grace. Opportunities were limited, however, by a tight budget, a low ceiling and a long list of fire regulations. Yasui saw light – the cheapest 'building block' – as the most effective solution to the multifaceted problem. His idea was to give customers the feeling that they had just awakened and were still blinded by the light of a new day, an unknown period of experiences exciting and different – very much like fashions by D'Grace. He began by installing white lighting on the walls and placing panels of translucent plastic in front of them. At certain spots the panelling projects from the walls to form display units. Applying the name D'Grace here and there with the use of a special film gives the panels yet another function: interior billboards. The brand name is incorporated into the aluminium floor as well. Yasui extended his lighting concept to columns at the entrance of the shop, which greet visitors like oversized lamps. The only wooden component is the counter. Clothing hangs from rails that seem to float along columns and walls. Focal points are curved displays of transparent plastic that can be grouped in any number of ways to amplify the existing space. Ultimately, however, the customer's attention is drawn to the merchandise. The space as a whole is not particularly calming; customers tend to blink and narrow their eyes to get used to the light. Precisely the effect that Yasui set out to create!

HIDEO YASUI ATELIER **189** POWERSHOP

SATIN DOLL

What the client wanted for this compact watch shop was a look of exclusivity. Amidst hordes of screaming retailers and flashing illuminated ads in the nightlife section of Tokyo's Shinjuku district, Hideo Yasui found himself confronted with a façade a mere 2 metres wide. To attract attention to the premises, he gave the narrow space an oval form. Customers step up, cross the threshold and find themselves standing on an aluminium floor that resembles loose duckboards. Straight ahead is a diagonally placed bench. Yasui combined the oblique line of this bench with indirect lighting built into floor and ceiling to make the room look somewhat wider. But the keyword to unravelling this mysterious space is 'curiosity'. Halogen spots illuminate antique watches housed in crystalline showcases. A minimal lighting scheme lends warmth to white-painted walls. By concealing the air-conditioning unit behind a convex oval component, Yasui also managed to create a cosy corner next to the counter. And a kitschy plush sofa is anchored in place by basic anti-slip flooring.

LA CIENEGA

In designing La Cienega in Matsumoto, again Hideo Yasui was faced with an elongated piece of land and a brief that asked for a shop, a stockroom and an office. The 165-square-metre space invited the designer to juggle daylight, split levels and optical illusions for a result that gives the narrow space an ambience of grandeur. Restricted to a minimum, the furnishings in this project are sometimes virtually invisible. Now and again Yasui used the glass cabinets and display cases to express his sense of playfulness. Aiming for a high degree of flexibility, he also designed a number of easy-to-move acrylic cabinets. Clothing which more or less levitates along the walls is illuminated by indirect lighting installed in the rails that support fashions on hangers. Indirect lighting throughout the outlet mimics daylight in a space without a single spotlight. Glass roof panels, centrally positioned, provide an abundance of natural light. The focus at La Cienega is on fashions by Atsuro Tayama and other young Japanese fashion designers. In terms of colour and size, the building fits quite naturally into the streetscape. What makes La Cienega special, however, are its two faces, both of which look out on shopping streets. A predominantly glass façade on the broader street displays a wonderful metal bulge that fronts an oval office virtually hovering in space. The opposite façade, also glass, tilts forward and provides a view of the store's two levels, as well as its softly undulating ceiling. Thanks to a highly transparent interior, Yasui's design effectively accentuates the form of the building.

FEMME ET MODE

Like 'the bed of an eel' is Hideo Yasui's slippery description of the site on which fashion shop Femme et Mode now stands. After studying the 8-metre-wide and 35-metre-deep location, Yasui adopted the 'museum principle' as the point of departure for his design. Standing at the entrance, the visitor can look deep into the interior of the boutique without really seeing what the space has to offer. Brighter light at the rear of the shop draws the customer up the stairs and into the outlet. Unable to use as much natural light as he prefers, Yasui illuminated the shop with the next best thing: indirect lighting. At the front of the shop, glass ceiling panels filter the artificial light. Farther back a triangular lighting element on the ceiling provides indirect lighting while also allowing natural light to enter the room, except on those winter days when a thick layer of snow on the roof blocks all outdoor light. Each level of the shop accommodates a different clothing brand: Femme et Mode's well-organised shops-in-a-shop carry merchandise by Yohji Yamamoto and Atsuro Tayama, among others. Beneath the retail space lie a stockroom and an office with a view of the rear garden. Yasui's design blends right in with its immediate surroundings. Observing the high street of provincial Yuzawa from a distance, you would have a hard time spotting Femme et Mode.

D'GRACE (SENDAI FORUS)

Hideo Yasui's second encounter with fashion label D'Grace – an abbreviation of Dazzling Grace – is, as requested by the client, a bit more serene. Although D'Grace again asked him to pursue an image of the more mature woman, Yasui interpreted the brief for this outlet as a light space based on an abstract impression of flowers. Transparent silk-screen prints of pastel petals decorate the glass display cases. The sweet, dreamy atmosphere created by these blossoms contrasts nicely with an austere aluminium floor and bright walls aglow with indirect lighting. Yasui reinforced the squareness of the space with the use of angular glass display cases. An air of transparency adds to the spacious feel of the compact boutique and focuses attention on the casual fashions, which currently feature the ever-popular look of denim.

DGRACE

TOKUJIN YOSHIOKA DESIGN
TOKUJIN YOSHIOKA

吉岡 徳仁

We're on the upper floor of Yoshioka's studio, which is part of his home. A wall unit functions as a partition between studio and living quarters, deftly hiding the kitchen and an oval wooden bathtub from the eyes of visitors. What at first glance looks like an ultramodern concrete dwelling proves to be a typically Japanese mix of concrete, glass and old wooden elements. A couple of bamboo plants outside the window sway in the breeze. The rooms are efficiently arranged and soberly simple, with the exception of a small, jam-packed office on the ground floor, in which four employees seem to have no more room than the parking space for the Mercedes 4WD parked outside. The most striking aspect of the building, however, is the wood, which not only functions as a cosmetic ornament but also forms the skeleton of the entire structure. Approaching the task as if playing with a child's building kit, Tokujin Yoshioka found an old barn out in the country, disassembled the weathered wooden carcass and put it back together on this small piece of land in the hip neighbourhood of Daikanyama. 'What a job,' sighs the designer, who sees the project as one of his greater challenges to date. Behind the apparent simplicity lies a complex jigsaw puzzle of sorts, a fine example of the way in which Yoshioka works.

A maquette in his office represents a more recent project: the Mori Building, a gallery-bookshop-café combination. A glazed façade 6 metres high and 22 metres long is the showpiece of the design. Yoshioka created windows that distort the view of the interior and, in so doing, give passers-by the impression that the floor inside is an inclined plane. The optical illusion makes both sculptures and visitors standing on this 'slope' vaguely discernible from a distance. It took an entire year to develop the special glass required. Several Japanese glass manufacturers found the experiment too risky. If the designer himself had had no prior knowledge of chemistry, the glass for this project may never have been created. 'I want people to scratch their heads and wonder how in the world it was done,' laughs Yoshioka, who loves to conjure up magic with spectacular materials for his oh-so-simple but powerful designs.

The idea of becoming a designer blossomed very early on. 'I must have been no more than six or seven when I fell in love with drawing,' says the thirty-something designer. 'My parents recognised a spark of talent and sent me to an industrial secondary school with a strong focus on the Bauhaus tradition. It's there that I learned to look inside myself for a way in which to develop a pure form. It was all very abstract; we weren't offered much practical experience.' After graduating from the Kuwasawa Design School, he began his career with furniture designer Shiro Kuramata. His work for Kuramata brought him in contact with fashion designer Issey Miyake, who asked Yoshioka to join his studio in 1988. 'I don't have much in common with the majority of fashion designers,' he says. 'Issey-san is an exception. He's had a tremendous influence on me. So has Kuramata for that matter, and I also admire the work of Frank Gehry.' In 1992 the young designer decided to take on freelance commissions, and in 2000 he set up his own company, Tokujin Yoshioka Design Office. In addition to space design, he's also active in the field of product design. His first interior project was the design of an Issey Miyake exhibition in Amsterdam's Stedelijk Museum, an event that launched a series of high-profile shows devoted to the fashion mogul. Yoshioka's installations for *Issey Miyake Making Things* – the title of a travelling exhibition held in Paris, New York and Tokyo – created quite a stir in the world of fashion and art. Clothes leaping through the air, artistic projections and museological decorations featuring futuristic fabrics made a visit to the show a buoyant but highly impressive experience. Sensors responded to the approach of visitors by setting objects in motion. Images projected on the floor of one room provided a step-by-step scenario of a Miyake design from conception to completion. Garments in the same space were displayed in illuminated glory. Education rubbed elbows with entertainment. 'Generally speaking, signs next to works of art in a museum are an important source of information,' Yoshioka explains. 'I wanted to eliminate all that bending forward and squinting, and let the visitor experience

'CLIENTS HAVE TO BE SOMEWHAT GUTSY, BECAUSE I WANT THE FREEDOM TO PLAY WITH MATERIALS THAT ARE NOT ALWAYS THE OBVIOUS CHOICES'

without words why Issey Miyake's designs and the fabrics he chooses are so unique.'

Whether the subject is an exhibition or a shop interior, Yoshioka's main objective is to surprise the observer – not in an overwhelming way, but subtly and in the details. His designs are characterised by the inventive execution of a simple idea. His concept for the HAAT shop, for example, is that of a space clad only in lighting effects. The lighting changes as the day goes on and is dependent, moreover, on the collection and the number of customers. The unsuspecting visitor has no idea that 700 LED lamps on the ceiling react to sensors installed at the entrance. Everyone who walks in, however, realises that 'something strange' is going on here. This type of strategy is Yoshioka's invisible trademark. In other designs, it might be a special layer of film on the shop window or lighting tucked away in a transparent tube.

An essential source of inspiration is technology. 'Technology implies the future,' he says, ' and I'm extremely curious about what the future holds in store, especially on a visual level. Technology and art are closely connected. I see the two as being virtually interchangeable, and that's an enormously fascinating idea.'

In his search for materials, Yoshioka goes a step farther than most retail designers. Considered by many as a genius in this area, he's been called the 'material boy', thanks to his experiments with unconventional combinations of materials. He's been known to impregnate glass, for example, with Indian sand, gravel or synthetic substances as a means of enhancing his designs.

Yoshioka does not wholeheartedly embrace the nickname he's been given. 'True, I'm always looking for new applications,' he admits, 'but the material must be functional as well.' He sees materials as the derivative of his original concept. 'It's like food. If you're a cook, you buy your vegetables from the person who cultivates them. But you can confer with him and let him know what you want in terms of size, taste and colour. As a designer, I do the same thing. I also need to know what's available.' This is an aspect of design that he analyses thoroughly. 'I'm totally into chemistry. I understand the composition of various materials,

and I like to mix them and come up with something new.' According to Yoshioka, when put into perspective, what he does is 'not terribly innovative'. When asked about the technical details of his work, he hesitates – copycats could be listening – and keeps his answer vague: 'I like materials that can communicate in some way or another and that can be enjoyed by everyone. Technological fireworks that only specialists can understand are not what I'm looking for. Whatever effect I achieve has to be fun for all, from tiny tots to senior citizens.'

Yoshioka subjects each client to his own selection process. 'First I find out if the client really wants to do something new. They have to be somewhat gutsy, because I want the freedom to play with materials that are not always the obvious choices. I try to avoid projects that involve a space aimed strictly at increasing sales. I'd rather do fewer shops and wait for those that allow me to be innovative. What's more, creating a sense of freshness and novelty that will last demands time. I do a lot of research, and despite the sometimes apparently simple results, a long process precedes many of my designs.'

At the moment, Yoshioka is concentrating on product design, but he expresses the desire to work on the interior of a small hotel. 'Not the whole interior,' he insists, 'but surprising accents like a special bathing area, for instance, or one or more art installations.' When asked about long-term plans, he says he wants to follow in the footsteps of his teacher, Kuramata, or in those of another eminent Japanese designer, Sori Yanagi, both all-rounders in their profession. As the winner of several international design awards, however, Yoshioka has already made a few footprints of his own.

TOKUJIN YOSHIOKA DESIGN
TOKUJIN YOSHIOKA

吉岡 徳仁

A-POC (AOYAMA)

LOCATION
**3-17-14 Minami Aoyama, Minato-ku,
Tokyo**
CLIENT
Issey Miyake
FLOOR AREA
221 m²
START DESIGN
November 1999
OPENING
18 February 2000
INTERIOR ARCHITECT
Tokujin Yoshioka
GENERAL CONSTRUCTOR
Ishimaru
LIGHTING DESIGN
Yamagiwa
FLOOR
mortar
WALL
acrylic emergent paint on glass fibre cloth
CEILING
aluminium exhaust panel (BMW)
WINDOW
glass
LIGHTING FIXTURES
halogen tubes
DISPLAY TABLES
glass, stainless steel
COUNTER
wood
SHOWCASE
stainless steel

PHOTOGRAPHY
Nacása & Partners

ISSEY MIYAKE

LOCATION
**Seibu 7F,
2-5 Yurakucho, Chuo-ku,
Tokyo**
CLIENT
Issey Miyake
FLOOR AREA
60 m²
START DESIGN
December 2001
OPENING
1 March 2001
INTERIOR ARCHITECT
Tokujin Yoshioka
GENERAL CONSTRUCTOR
Ishimaru
LIGHTING DESIGN
Max Ray, Endo
FLOOR
homogeneous vinyl tile
WALL
coloured glass
CEILING
acrylic emergent paint
LIGHTING FIXTURES
tubes (Max Ray), lights (Endo)
COUNTER
coloured glass
CHAIR
urethane

PHOTOGRAPHY
Nacása & Partners

HAAT

LOCATION
**1F,
4-21-29 Minami Aoyama, Minato-ku,
Tokyo**
CLIENT
Issey Miyake
FLOOR AREA
163 m²
START DESIGN
April 2001
OPENING
13 July 2001
INTERIOR ARCHITECT
Tokujin Yoshioka
GENERAL CONSTRUCTOR
Ishimaru
LIGHTING DESIGN
LED / Colorkinetics, Endo
FLOOR
mortar
WALL
acrylic emergent paint
CEILING
acrylic emergent paint
WINDOW
glass
LIGHTING FIXTURES
LED tube lights
SYSTEM FURNITURE
Line system (One by One)
CHAIR
Primate (Castiglione)
DISPLAY TABLES
steel
COUNTER
steel, glass (first floor); steel (basement)
SHOWCASE
steel

PHOTOGRAPHY
Nacása & Partners

A-POC (OSAKA)

LOCATION
**Namba City, B1F,
5-1-60, Namba, Chuo-ku,
Osaka**
CLIENT
Issey Miyake
FLOOR AREA
115 m²
START DESIGN
July 2001
OPENING
5 October 2001
INTERIOR ARCHITECT
Tokujin Yoshioka
GENERAL CONSTRUCTOR
Ishimaru
LIGHTING DESIGN
Endo
FLOOR
white painted concrete
WALL
polycarbonate
CEILING
acrylic emergent paint
LIGHTING FIXTURES
Endo
SYSTEM FURNITURE
Line System (One by One)
WORK TABLE
Corian, chrome
COUNTER
polycarbonate, steel

PHOTOGRAPHY
Nacása & Partners

TOKUJIN YOSHIOKA DESIGN
TOKUJIN YOSHIOKA DESIGN
TOKUJIN YOSHIOKA DESIGN
TOKUJIN YOSHIOKA DESIGN
TOKUJIN YOSHIOKA DESIGN
TOKUJIN YOSHIOKA DESIGN
TOKUJIN YOSHIOKA DESIGN
TOKUJIN YOSHIOKA DESIGN
TOKUJIN YOSHIOKA DESIGN
TOKUJIN YOSHIOKA DESIGN
TOKUJIN YOSHIOKA DESIGN
TOKUJIN YOSHIOKA DESIGN
TOKUJIN YOSHIOKA DESIGN
TOKUJIN YOSHIOKA DESIGN
TOKUJIN YOSHIOKA DESIGN
TOKUJIN YOSHIOKA DESIGN
TOKUJIN YOSHIOKA DESIGN
TOKUJIN YOSHIOKA DESIGN
TOKUJIN YOSHIOKA DESIGN
TOKUJIN YOSHIOKA DESIGN
TOKUJIN YOSHIOKA DESIGN
TOKUJIN YOSHIOKA DESIGN
TOKUJIN YOSHIOKA DESIGN
TOKUJIN YOSHIOKA DESIGN
TOKUJIN YOSHIOKA DESIGN
TOKUJIN YOSHIOKA DESIGN
TOKUJIN YOSHIOKA DESIGN
TOKUJIN YOSHIOKA DESIGN
TOKUJIN YOSHIOKA DESIGN
TOKUJIN YOSHIOKA DESIGN
TOKUJIN YOSHIOKA DESIGN
TOKUJIN YOSHIOKA DESIGN
TOKUJIN YOSHIOKA DESIGN
TOKUJIN YOSHIOKA DESIGN
TOKUJIN YOSHIOKA DESIGN
TOKUJIN YOSHIOKA DESIGN
TOKUJIN YOSHIOKA DESIGN
TOKUJIN YOSHIOKA DESIGN
TOKUJIN YOSHIOKA DESIGN
TOKUJIN YOSHIOKA DESIGN
TOKUJIN YOSHIOKA DESIGN
TOKUJIN YOSHIOKA DESIGN
TOKUJIN YOSHIOKA DESIGN
TOKUJIN YOSHIOKA DESIGN
TOKUJIN YOSHIOKA DESIGN
TOKUJIN YOSHIOKA DESIGN
TOKUJIN YOSHIOKA DESIGN
TOKUJIN YOSHIOKA DESIGN
TOKUJIN YOSHIOKA DESIGN
TOKUJIN YOSHIOKA DESIGN
TOKUJIN YOSHIOKA DESIGN
TOKUJIN YOSHIOKA DESIGN
TOKUJIN YOSHIOKA DESIGN
TOKUJIN YOSHIOKA DESIGN
TOKUJIN YOSHIOKA DESIGN
TOKUJIN YOSHIOKA DESIGN
TOKUJIN YOSHIOKA DESIGN
TOKUJIN YOSHIOKA DESIGN
TOKUJIN YOSHIOKA DESIGN
TOKUJIN YOSHIOKA DESIGN
TOKUJIN YOSHIOKA DESIGN
TOKUJIN YOSHIOKA DESIGN
TOKUJIN YOSHIOKA DESIGN
TOKUJIN YOSHIOKA DESIGN
TOKUJIN YOSHIOKA DESIGN
TOKUJIN YOSHIOKA DESIGN
TOKUJIN YOSHIOKA DESIGN
TOKUJIN YOSHIOKA DESIGN
TOKUJIN YOSHIOKA DESIGN

TOKUJIN YOSHIOKA DESIGN
9-1 DAIKANYAMA-CHO, SHIBUYA-KU, TOKYO, 150-0034 JAPAN
T +81 (0)3-5428-0830 F +81 (0)3-5428-0835
E TOKUJIN3AOL.COM WWW.TOKUJIN.COM

A-POC (AOYAMA)

Top-fashion designer Issey Miyake took his renowned and ingenious treatment of fabric a step further when he introduced the A-POC line. Sewing machines are virtually nonexistent in the making of these designs. Advanced computer technology is used to mould the seams directly into the stretch-cotton material. The result is a soft cylinder about 2 metres long from which the customer can cut (or have cut) an item of clothing of a certain length and shape with no frayed edges. The result is A-POC – A Piece Of Cloth. Elaborating on the concept of moulding, Yoshioka created a shop interior in which both ceiling and columns are covered with moulded material. German carmaker BMW produced the aluminium moulds, which partially block the view of robust

beams and columns and, at the same time, accentuate the rather low ceiling. Normally the material is used to make mufflers and other automotive components purposely hidden from view. The shop also accommodates the atelier for Miyake's A-POC concept. Clearly part of the retail establishment, it is separated from the rest of the space by no more than a glass partition. White-jacketed designers in a laboratory-like setting emphasise the high-tech image of the brand. A large worktable in the 'shopping zone' quite deliberately displays no sign of professional activity. After making a purchase, the customer can take a pair of scissors and, as the final link in the manufacturing process, use this table to tailor her own piece of cloth.

ISSEY MIYAKE

On an upper level of a typical Japanese department store in Yurakucho, a plain white box accommodates another Issey Miyake boutique. Fashions on the walls complement a central display of milk glass and stainless steel. What could have been a run-of-the-mill shop has been saved by a tubular lighting design installed above the hangers. Like a snake – or, less metaphorically, like an illuminated air-conditioning conduit – the tube meanders through the shop. Where does the light come from? A reflective, semitransparent film? T bulbs inside the tube? Is the serpent a complicated high-tech device or just a clever trick? Designer Tokujin Yoshioka remains tight-lipped when asked such questions. In any case, the monster is intriguing. Yoshioka introduced his tubular lighting concept in previous plans for the offices of mobile-telecom titan NTT-X, where he opened the ceiling and installed a fascinating network of luminous tubing rather than subjecting office workers to the monotony of a systems-built ceiling. In this brightly lit Miyake shop, however, the wandering tube seems more decorative than functional.

HAAT

Located on the same street as flagship stores belonging to Miyake, Yohji Yamamoto, Dolce & Gabbana, Commes des Garçons and Prada, the shop that Tokujin Yoshioka designed for Issey Miyake's folklore-inspired line is anything but ethnic. HAAT's wholly glazed shop front offers a clear but sobering view of the retail interior. Keeping in mind the tautly transparent ambience of other Miyake shops, here Yoshioka relied strictly on the effects produced by lighting to achieve the look he wanted. White walls and a rather rough concrete floor make a nice backdrop for his colourful accents. The fluorescent orange walls of a small corridor leading to the stockroom subtly reflect light into the sterile space. Spanning the entire length of the shop, a broad band of tiny lights runs across the ceiling and along the wall, gradually, almost imperceptibly, changing colour. Simple yet effective. After closing hours the cool space is bathed in a warm red glow. Fitting rooms are tucked behind a milk-glass wall used to project images that express the mood generated by the current collection. Connecting ground floor and basement levels are metal steps with anti-skid treads and a railing made of ordinary steel cable. Alternating lights on a broad cylindrical element downstairs are a big hit with the kids, who sit on a nearby chair staring in wonder at the fascinating parade of colours passing by.

A-POC (OSAKA)

Bubbling with spherical shapes, the façade of this Issey Miyake A-POC shop bears no resemblance at all to the exterior of its subdued and austere sister in Aoyama, Tokyo. A relationship to the earlier A-POC shop does exist, however. Here Yoshioka continues the moulding theme that characterises these fashions. This outlet is located below ground level, in one of Osaka's famous subterranean shopping paradises. Although Yoshioka installed various convex-moulded polycarbonate elements on the façade, the interior is the epitome of simplicity. An industrial-looking ironing board behind a glass wall evokes the image of a sewing atelier. And again, as in Aoyama, a large worktable free of employees dominates the space while waiting for a customer to lay out her purchase and whip it into the desired shape and style. Rollneck sweater? A V neck perhaps? A few snips of the shears and the choice is made, on the spot. Here at A-POC, the customer has the final say. When she leaves the store, she carries with her a piece of cloth that is unique.

THE AUTHOR

Carolien van Tilburg is a Dutch journalist and media producer who has lived in Japan since 1995. Thanks to an avid interest in the fields of architecture and design, she has become a regular contributor to *Frame*. One of her major projects was the compilation of a monograph on Klein Dytham architecture. A monograph on Japanese design office Curiosity will be published in the autumn of 2002.

COLOPHON

POWERSHOP
New Japanese Retail Design

PUBLISHERS
Frame Publishers
www.framemag.com
Birkhäuser – Publishers for Architecture
www.birkhauser.ch

WRITTEN BY
Carolien van Tilburg

COMPILED BY
Frame magazine,
Carolien van Tilburg and
Yoichi Yasuoka/Memex

GRAPHIC DESIGN
Roelof Mulder

COPY EDITING
Donna de Vries-Hermansader,
Billy Nolan

TRANSLATION
InOtherWords
(Donna de Vries-Hermansader)

PRODUCTION
Tessa Blokland/*Frame* magazine

COLOUR REPRODUCTION
Graphic Link

PRINTING
Hoonte Bosch & Keuning

DISTRIBUTION
Benelux, China, Japan, Korea and Taiwan
ISBN 90-806445-3-6
Frame Publishers
Lijnbaansgracht 87
NL-1015 GZ Amsterdam
The Netherlands
www.framemag.com

All other countries
ISBN 3-7643-6626-5
Birkhäuser – Publishers for Architecture
P.O. Box 133
CH-4010 Basel
Switzerland
Member of the BertelsmannSpringer
Publishing Group
www.birkhauser.ch

© 2002 Frame
© 2002 Birkhäuser

A CIP catalogue record for this book is available from the Library of Congress, Washington D.C., USA.

Deutsche Bibliothek Cataloging-in-Publication Data
PowerShop : [new japanese retail design] / Frame. [Written by Carolien van Tilburg]. - Basel ; Boston ; Berlin : Birkhäuser; Amsterdam : BIS-Publ., 2002

ISBN 3-7643-6626-5
ISBN 90-806445-3-6

Printed on acid-free paper produced from chlorine-free pulp. TCF ∞
Printed in the Netherlands
987654321